A Fairy Find begins with the discovery of a cache of wands. Not only does this provide evidence that the sprites are at large, it also opens the door onto a parallel universe in which we humans exist purely for the amusement of our fairy keepers and reveals that our continued existence hangs by a gossamer thread of fairy whim. Using happenstance images and curious captions, Andrew Lanyon offers a tantalising glimpse of the tiny, capricious creatures that pull our strings, trip us up and bend us to their mischievous ends.

Born in 1947, ANDREW LANYON is a painter, publisher, author and film-maker. His work has been acquired by public and private collections including the V&A in London and MOMA in New York. He lives in Cornwall with his family at the end of a dirt track.

A FAIRY FIND

Including

A CACHE OF WANDS
THE DREAM MIDWIVES
THE FAIRY WARS

by
Our Man in Fairyland

Published by Portobello Books Ltd 2006

Portobello Books Ltd
Eardley House
4 Uxbridge Street
Notting Hill Gate
London W8 7SY, UK

First published in three volumes by Andrew Lanyon
in limited editions in 2005

A CIP catalogue record is available from the British Library

9 8 7 6 5 4 3 2 1

ISBN 1 84627 061 8
13-digit ISBN 978 1 84627 061 1

www.portobellobooks.com

Designed by Clare Skeats
Typeset in Adobe Caslon by Clare Skeats
Printed and bound in China by Compass Press

To the memory of my grandfather, Colonel St John Browne, who wrote under the pseudonym 'SINJAB' in *Blackwood's* magazine, but whose writings to his children, on leaves, as if from the fairies, may have had more long-lasting effects . . .

For our daughter Rosa who crossed to France on a 'fairy boat' and for our son Sam who aged three saw a fairy fly out of its burrow.

A CACHE OF WANDS

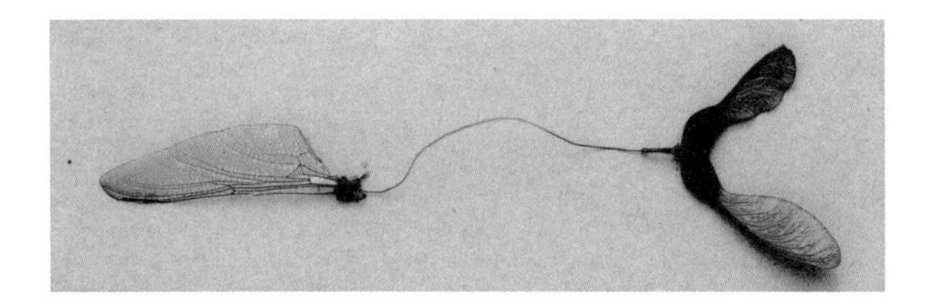

Fairy wand

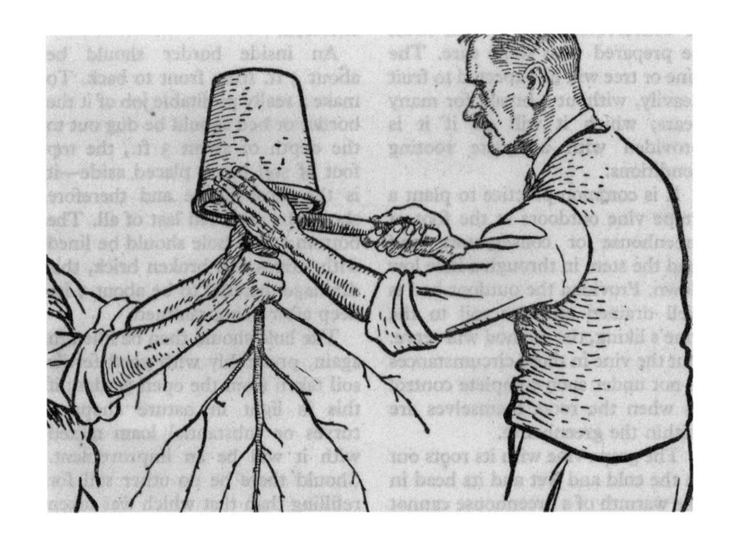

It is really no use two grown men thinking they can catch a fairy.

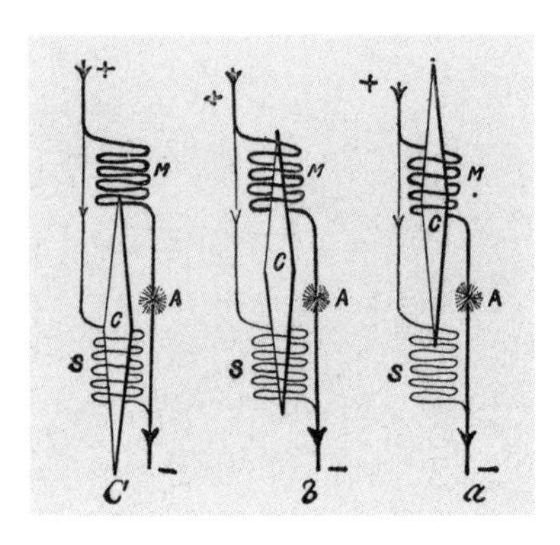

Fairy snares (set)

For centuries fairies have displayed great slipperiness at evading capture, in spite of the combined guile of the entire agricultural community. While pressed flowers and leaves sometimes flutter from old bibles when one shakes them, banknotes and squashed fairies never seem to.

Because they are so elusive, people sometimes whisper that fairies do not exist. Farmers, however, know that they do. But then farmers could not function without scapegoats. The usual things that farmers blame, such as an inclement air stream, the price of barbed wire, an influx of foreign food or locusts, are all undependable and so they have come to rely on fairies. And farmers will go to endless lengths to root out the sprites that they know are living off their land.

Laying a fairy trap

Fairy fumigation

The fairy catcher

Poison

Signs of fairies

Those who do not believe in fairies do not tend to go out of their way to inform farmers about their non-belief, for instance by proselytising at cattle auctions. Anyone who desires to go on eating is well advised not to interfere with farmers or their methods. Anyway, if farmers want to spend time chasing fairies, does it really matter? Even farmers need hobbies and you honestly can't see them making balsa aircraft or collecting stamps.

Fairy tracking

Fairies are nothing if not quick. Both speed of movement and thought are vital to their survival. But there is reliable evidence that they have also developed considerable mimicry skills.

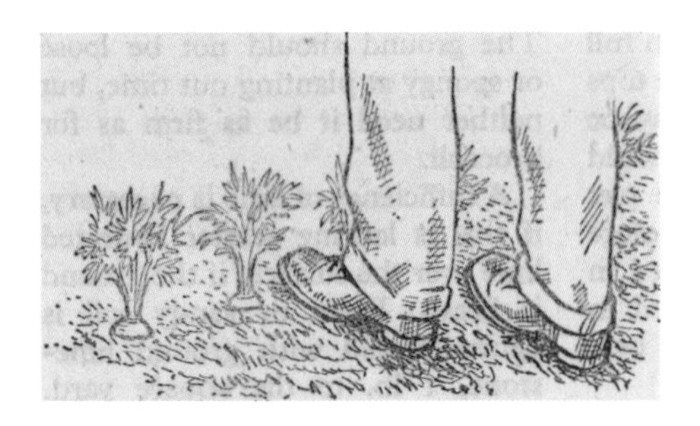

Fairies pretending to be carrot tops and remaining perfectly still (difficult for fairies)

Several hundred fairies pretending to be tins jangling on a farmer's wife's washing line just to annoy her (and therefore him)

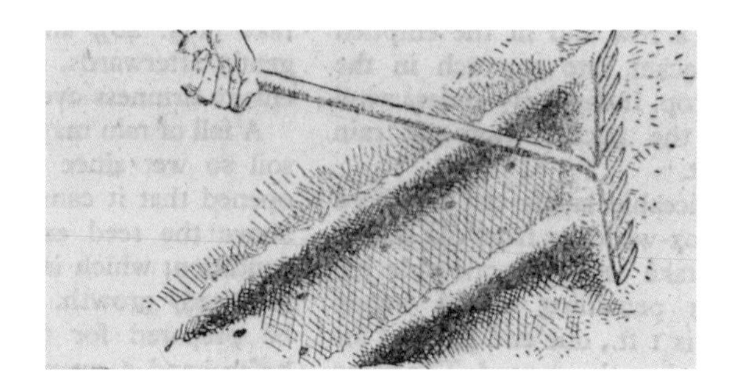

Waiting to knock a fairy senseless as it emerges from its burrow

To drown a lot of fairies at once

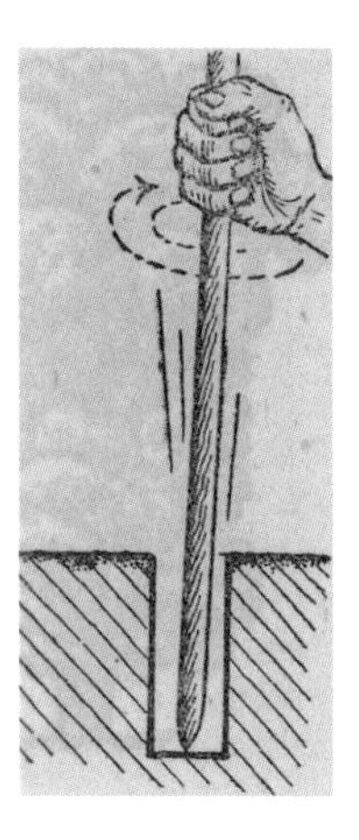

To panic a fairy colony

No one has ever caught a fairy or even found a dead one. Maybe they live forever.

Incontrovertible proof of the existence of fairies

The longevity of fairies infuriates the agricultural types one sees leaning on gates, gates which one imagines might not remain upright for long should the farmers decide not to lean on them. Farmers are forever pursuing pests as well as jealously guarding their crops from beetles, crows and small boys or herding here and there hundreds of pets. The farmer knows all these things have predictable life cycles which helps him keep them alive until he decides it is the perfect moment for them to die, thereby turning them into cash, which is useful for grubbing out hedges and trees, etc. Farmers know that fairies live and that therefore, like everything else, they must die. So it is a constant source of annoyance when they do not.

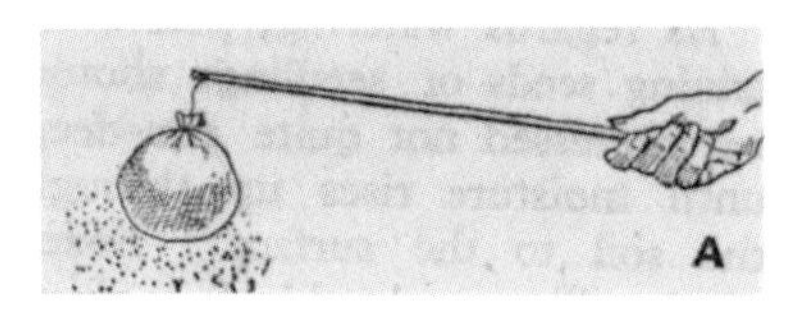

One of a large range of devices sold to assist farmers in warding off fairies or luring them closer for extermination

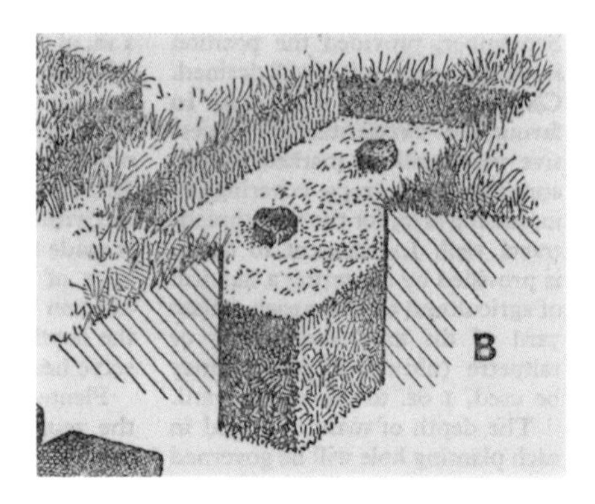

A fairy optical illusion. It is just this sort of thing that drives farmers wild, so wild that they take it out on their wives, children, neighbours, tractors, livestock and crops.

Three fairies stifling laughter at a farmer using a rake the wrong way up

It is a common enough sight to see a farmer pulling a plough with a tractor (or horses) for days or even weeks, turning over his entire property to find a single fairy. He knows it is there. The evidence is all around him.

And so this ancient symbiotic relationship between fairy and farmer continues without any harm being done to either species. In fact such an old relationship would probably continue even if it was proven beyond any shadow of doubt that there are no such things as farmers.

But we have reliable evidence that one afternoon in 1938 an archaeologist observed half a dozen fairies whittling wands on a knoll. They were only about half an inch high and did not have wings. Well, one did. But as it was so hot he slipped them off like a coat. After a while the six of them just wandered away. Returning to the knoll the next morning, the archaeologist discovered a cache of wands nearby and what turned out to be the remains of a fairy city.

The archaeologist died many years ago but what he found was rediscovered last year in some shoe boxes in the attic of an old house. From the excavated artefacts and from the drawings the archaeologist made of the fairy flats and apartments, certain revolutionary conclusions may be drawn concerning what drives fairies and how this relates to us. For there is, it seems, an important link between the various fairy kingdoms and our own, a connection which no one has hitherto suspected, one which sheds a good deal of light on who we are and what on earth we are doing here.

Sketch of a fairy wand

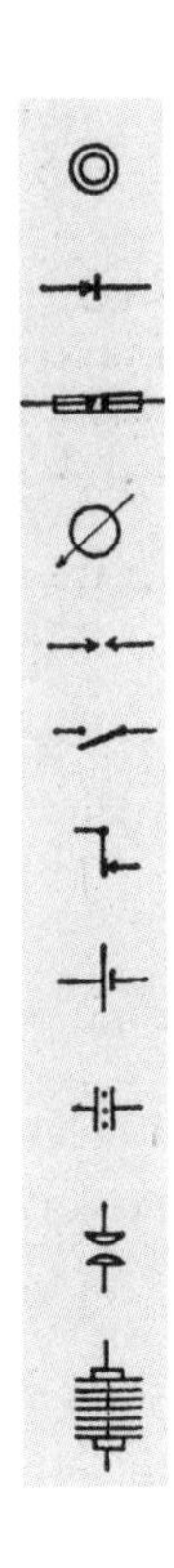

Signs left by fairies for other fairies

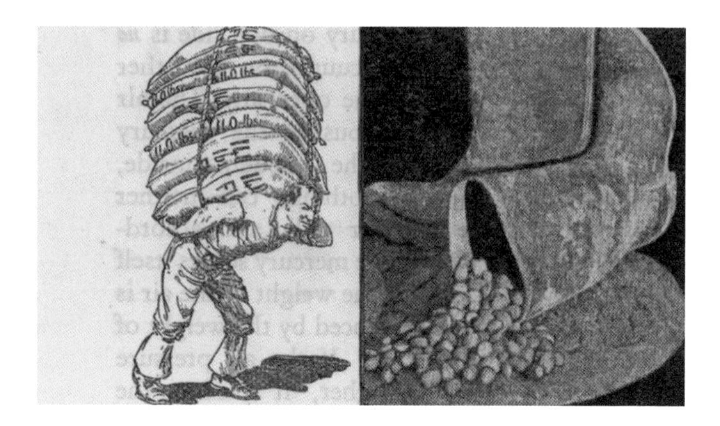

The kind of ride a fairy finds irresistible
and a typical fairy trick

Before we look at the conclusions the archaeologist came to, it is worthwhile noting two things about fairies, two things which every culture has come to associate with the little folk: flight and mischief.

With regard to flight, angels, who also have wings, are quite probably a type of fairy. Christians once argued about how many angels might alight on a pin head, so it has even been recognised by the clergy that angels can be diminutive. Fairies, piskies and elves are all mischievous but their teasing never reaches beyond threat. For example we would not expect the big fairy opposite to actually dispatch the other satanic elf. They are just romping.

Spot the 10,000 fairies

While fairies and their kind are numerous and live in burrows, angels are far scarcer and dwell above, in the sky, only dropping in briefly. They tend to be serious, as if on urgent business like lawyers delivering injunctions. Although angels lack the mischievousness associated with their underground cousins, the similarities that exist between fairies and angels suggest that they are both variants of a single species, less different in fact than our own Inuit and Aborigine.

Anyway, all fairies are perfect mimics so they are capable of presenting themselves as either a large singular messenger or a small multiple elf.

'Having first drowned your fairy, take no chances, because fairies are masters at feigning death.'
FAIRY TRAP CATALOGUE HANDBOOK

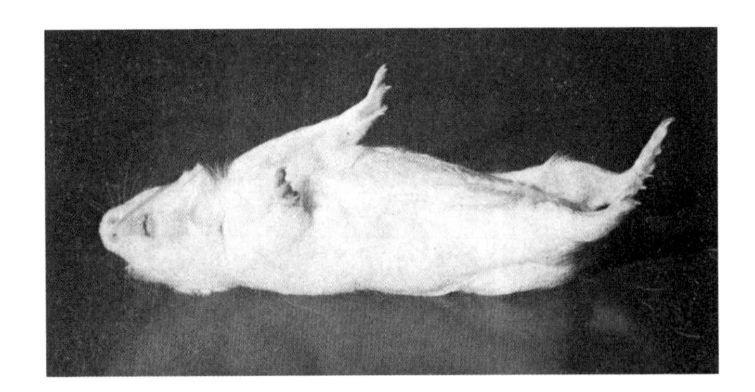

The skill perfected by fairies at feigning death is a skill they have been known to pass on to other creatures, like the guinea pig opposite, who is only pretending to be dead in the hope that its child owner will shriek and run to its mother, leaving the cage door wide open. But no child would be fooled by that look. Anyone can tell it is a beginner.

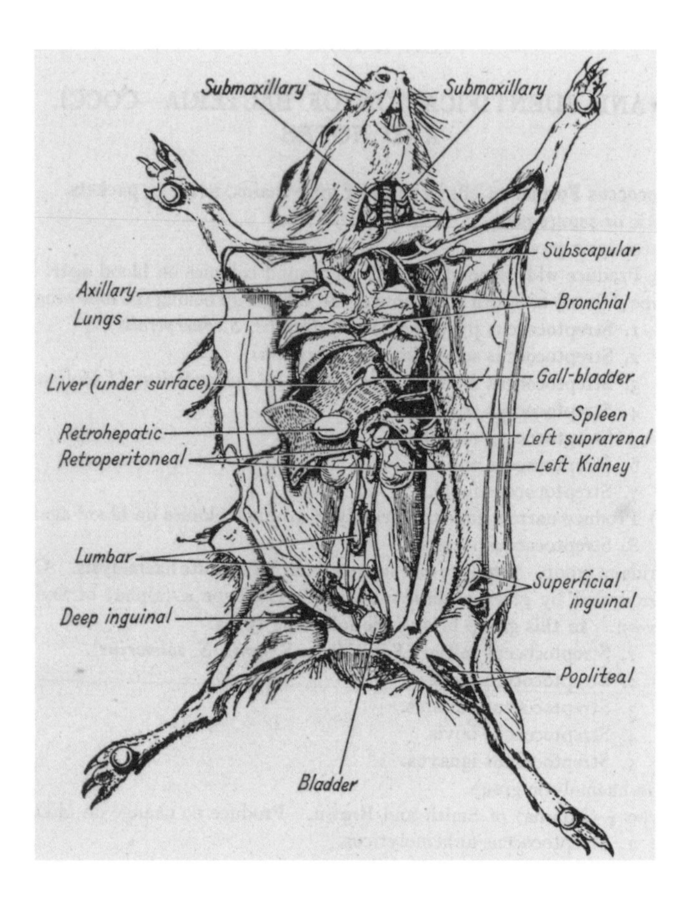

Unlike this guinea pig, who is definitely dead.

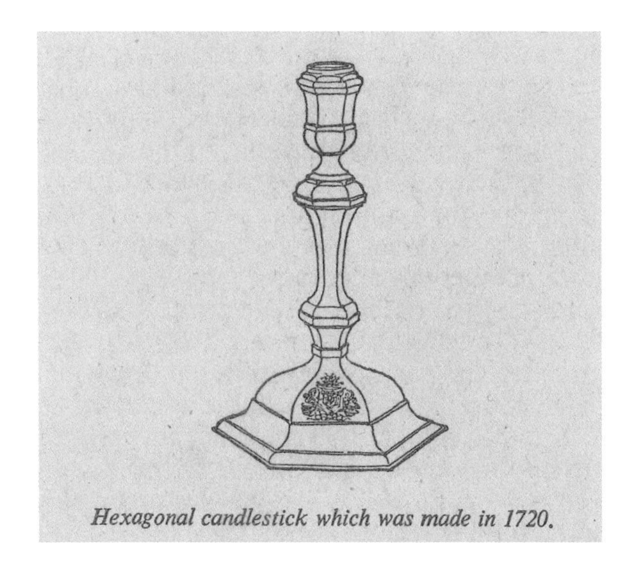

Hexagonal candlestick which was made in 1720.

... 'and' (the caption about the candlestick ought to continue) 'was invaded by a large colony of very small fairies the very same year.'

Scottish skittleball teapot, 1725.

Within five years the fairy colony had spread from the hexagonal candlestick to the Scottish skittleball teapot, evolving a larger and more decorative city layout.

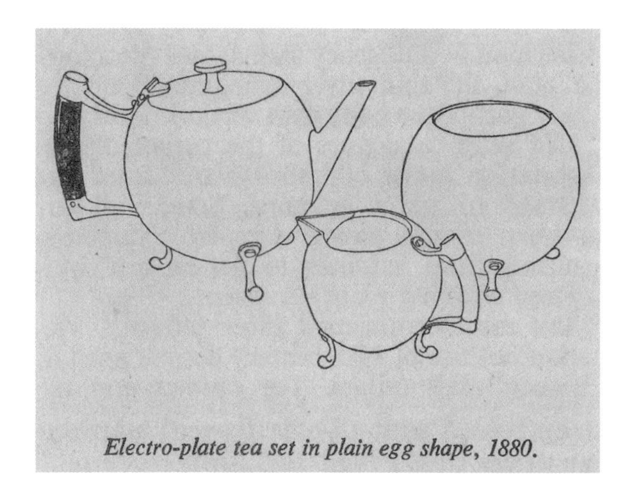

Electro-plate tea set in plain egg shape, 1880.

By the 1880s fairies had moved on from tableware, to populate antique rococo revival snuff boxes instead . . .

Rococo revival snuff box with high relief ornament, 1846.

There appears to be a chronological discrepancy here.
Fairies love creating chronological discrepancies.
But that's another story . . .

Whilst fairy cities can look like anything fairies want them to, so too can fairies. The difference is that if a city is built to look like a teapot, it cannot easily be altered. But individual fairies can change into almost anything, instantaneously. Here for example is a fairy imitating a dog irritating a motorist.

For a long time this was believed to be the King and Queen of the fairies. But forensic advances have revealed it to be just any old fairy a moment later.

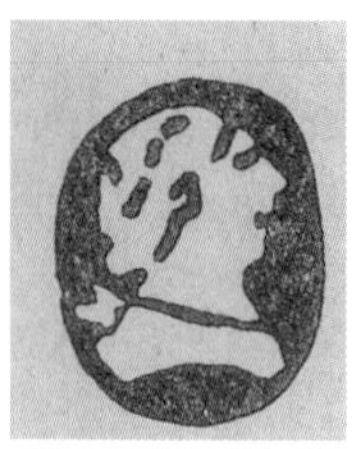

A perfectly ordinary straight line bent by fairies

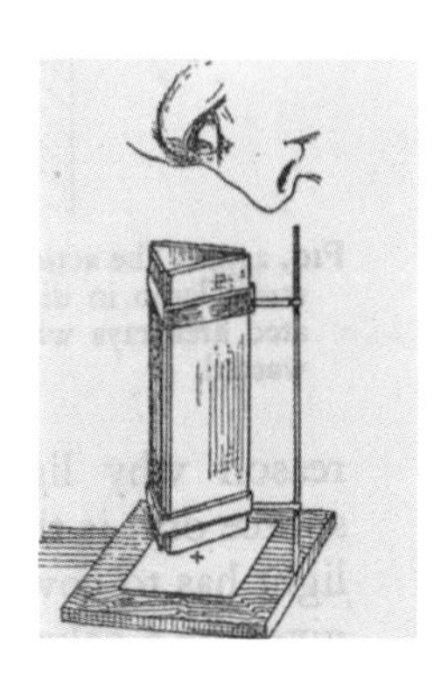

A scientist observing a fairy imitating an x

A fairy changing its size

Fairies can appear microscopic one moment, as large as a person the next. If they see a bit of old pottery thrown out in a hedge which would obviously make the most perfect summer house, they simply change their size to suit. If they should come to really love this summer house and desire to live in it all the year round, but suddenly one afternoon have a dozen children, all they have to do is shrink a bit, say from half an inch to a quarter, and they will all still have plenty of room. As the young fairies grow, the whole family will shrink again to compensate.

It is not such a large step from this observation regarding fairies adapting their size in order to suit the things they find, to one which suggests that a long time ago fairies realised that rather than make a lot of things themselves, they need only create two humans the once and then humans could make everything for them ever after. Final proof that we were actually created by fairies came with the exhumation of an entire bone factory in which creatures of all shapes and sizes had been in a state of manufacture.

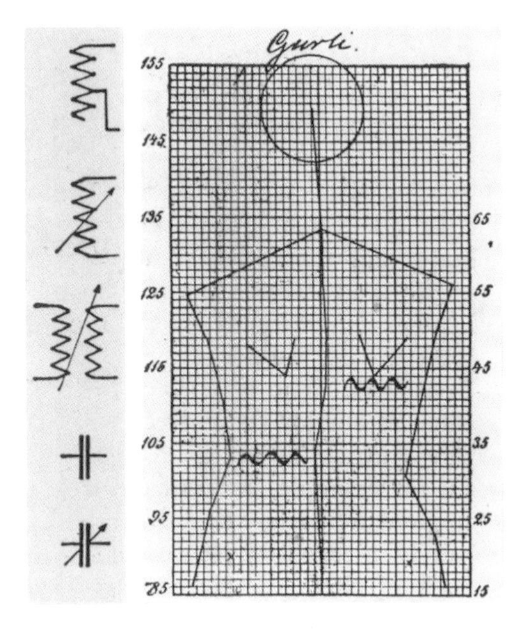

Fairy bone-knitting stitches and a sketch for a human

Fairies simply construct a figure out of bone, leave it on a shelf in the propagation room and introduce tiny organisms, which evolve rapidly into all the working parts.

It is quite a turnabout to consider that we have not been made by one large god but by lots and lots of minuscule elves.

Fairies manufacture pheromones from a number of ingredients. Tulip bulbs, for instance.

In order to maintain control over all their creations, particularly humans, fairies dreamed up pheromones. And it is with these that to this day they control our breeding, making sure that we continue to behave badly. It is by this means that fairies have provided themselves with a perfect model of how not to evolve.

Though fairies have fashioned every creature for their own amusement or for a bet or a dare, it is humans who above all provide them with the most useful and entertaining model of absurdity . . .

But no system is foolproof and now and then we throw up someone whom fairies must eliminate quickly or breed out, someone like the Victorian chef who came up with some recipes for fairies:

> *Wash the fairies and throw away all that float upon the water. Soak for twelve hours. Salt slightly and bring to the boil. Simmer till tender and arrange symmetrically.*
>
> *Take half a dozen sound fairies and peel and slice them thickly. Sprinkle with melted butter and bake for ten minutes. Serve on fried croûtons.*

Whenever they create new species, fairies are always extremely careful to ensure that none of them develops an appetite for fairies. But just to make sure, fairies themselves exude an aura of inedibility. When it came to goats, however, something went horribly wrong.

One dread day in the fairy calendar several fairies went missing and alarm bells began sounding throughout all the fairy kingdoms. After further disappearances, a goat was caught in the act, the remains of a fairy found in its mouth. Goats had discovered to their delight that by biting through a fairy's bitter dry husk, inside was a deliciously succulent centre. Rather than wipe out this devilishly horned, tailed and cloven-hoofed 'sheep deviant', fairies turned poisonous. After some goats found themselves flat on their backs with their hooves in the air, the message began to sink in and fairies relaxed once more into their normally exalted state of annoying invincibility which so infuriates farmers and goats.

Beating fairies towards a net

Fairies get a lot of ideas for their antics by observing humans. They enjoy predicting what it is people will do given a set of circumstances like a hat nailed to a hat stand or an awful lot of stairs. Being highly proficient mimics, fairies will amuse themselves 'playing people' for ages. For example the doorbell will go in a fairy semi, as a fairy carrying a narrow cardboard box arrives yelling 'pizza delivery'. This always sends the other fairies hysterical. Or several fairies will turn up at another fairy's place, each carrying a large square cardboard box with a window cut in it. Then they'll all get inside their cardboard TVs and talk for about four hours without connecting.

Little do those people who develop theories about fate governing our actions realise that we are subject to the urges and whims not of fate, but of fairies.

Fairies have not wasted a moment evolving language. This has saved a lot of misunderstanding as well as ink. It has also eliminated the need for philosophy, literature, history, SF, chat shows, quizzes, verse, prose, runes and farce. But fairies often gesticulate and they find the optional wings quite useful for adding nuance (unless there is a high wind). When fairies speak, it is always onomatopoeic. In other words they remember the sounds made by a human observed saying something. Because fairies have no language (to speak of) they do not fall victim to the pitfalls of logic, reason, meaning and belief.

Fairies observe that 'belief' is chiefly wielded by those humans who wish to control large numbers of others through fear. Fairies just have to laugh. Laughter is everything to them. There is nothing else they do half as much. They do not even eat, but breathe in all the nutrients they need. This means they do not waste time having to hunt, grow food, weed, fish, shop, cook, say grace, chew, swallow, chide their young for bolting food or tipping a chair, wash up, dry up, belch or foul the ground. Nor do fairies waste any time falling in love.

There are two chief areas of pleasure for fairies: laughter and sex. Though fairies hugely enjoy sex, it is no use whatsoever when it comes to reproduction. This they do by laughing. A fairy will be walking along one day and suddenly think of something funny and have a laughing fit. While in the throes of this paroxysm of mirth, out pops a perfect little fairy. Fairies consider this to be a far better arrangement than 'sex between parents', because the fairy system guarantees happy healthy offspring. There is no need for fairies to force themselves on one another or engage in the old human pastimes of abducting females or of having to procreate stealthily, for example while the other is asleep or drunk.

GENESIS.
Chap.XXXIV.V.26.
Dinah Defiled

Above all, the 'single fairy parent's' state of mind is never in question. Since humans only get half a set of genitalia each, a lot of time and energy is taken up checking for a reasonable fit. Fairies, however, get the whole kit, half being at the back, the other half in front. Hence all the fairy rings.

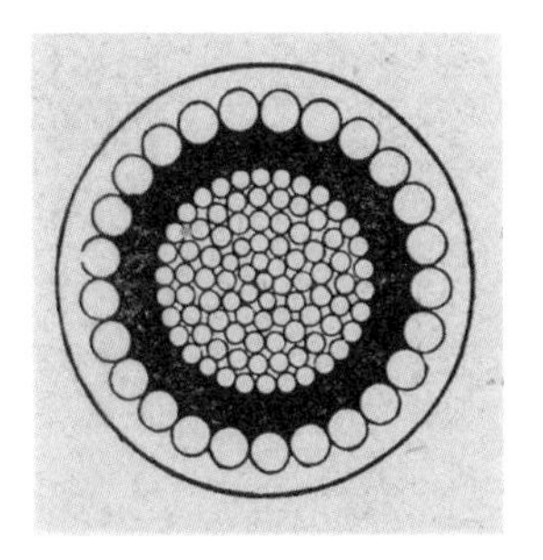

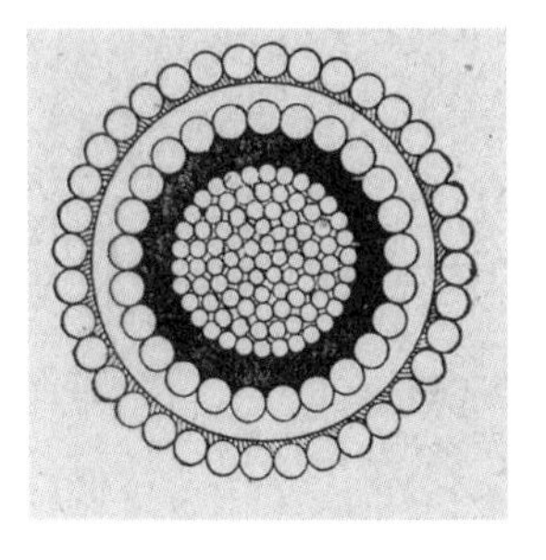

Fairy rings

Sixteen successive layers of plastering on a fairy nursery, from which it has been ascertained that fairies laugh an awful lot

All fairy youths are obliged to pass a test of courage. This involves the stealing of human teeth. Brave fairies have been known to knock a tooth out of an awake adult and some will even steal a child and leave the tooth. Brought up by fairies, these pilfered children have become the giants of legend.

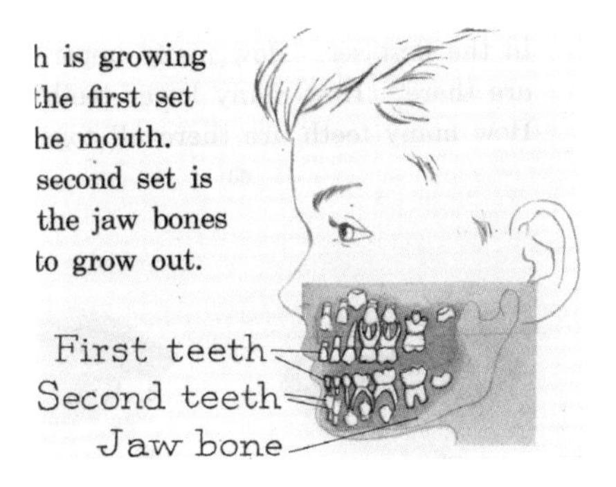

Fairies in the act of taking teeth

No fairy has ever experienced an identity crisis, because all fairies are called either Tinkerbill or Tinkerbell, according to whether they are moving backwards or forwards. A simple change in direction or size solves all fairy problems.

Fairies surfing

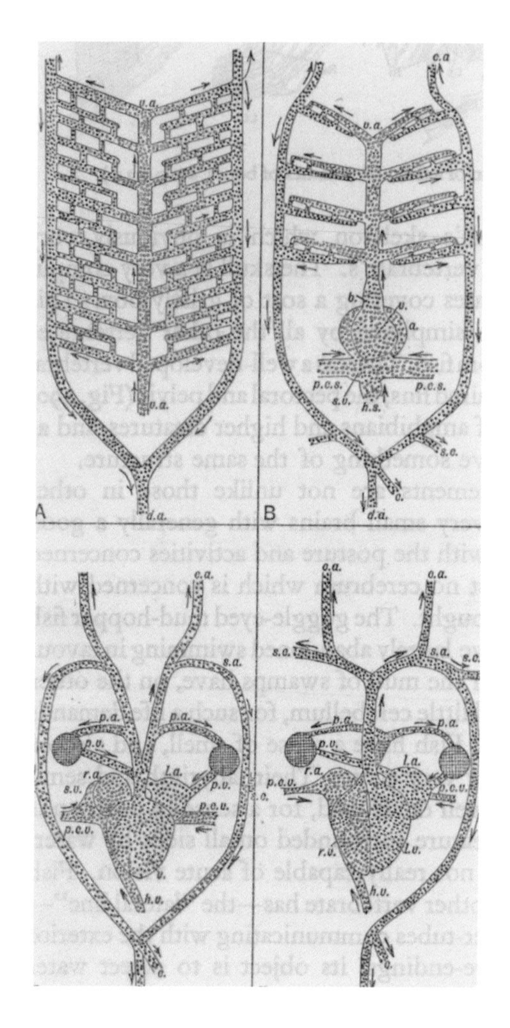

Four fairy cities

A bit of a human city and a bit of a fairy city

Because fairies are weightless, their rooms are arranged higgledy piggledy, at every angle. When the first fairy city was excavated it was not at first realised that below it there were other cities. Fairy cities are often upside down, i.e. fairies build downwards. They observe us digging up soil, carting it miles, turning it into bricks which we then have to pile up into the air, and they just have to laugh . . .

The bell-jar method

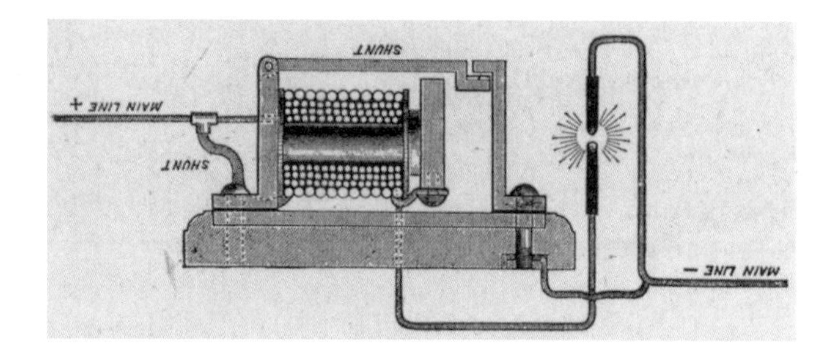

Fairy electrocutor

One of a dozen wands thought to have been made by fairies and found in a field near Zennor in west Cornwall in 1938

The famous 'notched wand' with its day and night references to daydreams and nightmares. The notches may refer to successes the fairy sorcerer achieved with this wand.

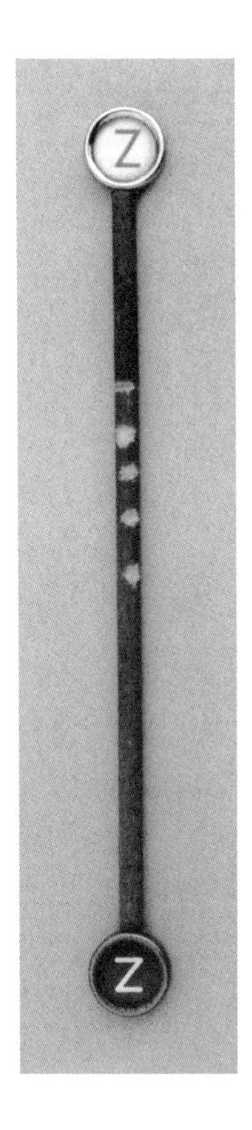
Z
Z

According to notes left by the archaeologist, the fairy wand opposite refers to the way in which fairies dream up new species, which is by throwing shadows on their burrow walls on winter evenings, amidst a good deal of raucous laughter.

Fairy hands are no different from human hands, only smaller and without bones. In fact fairy anatomy is almost identical to human, though a fairy's framework is closer to that of an insect than a mammal, with an insect's infuriating lightness and speed.

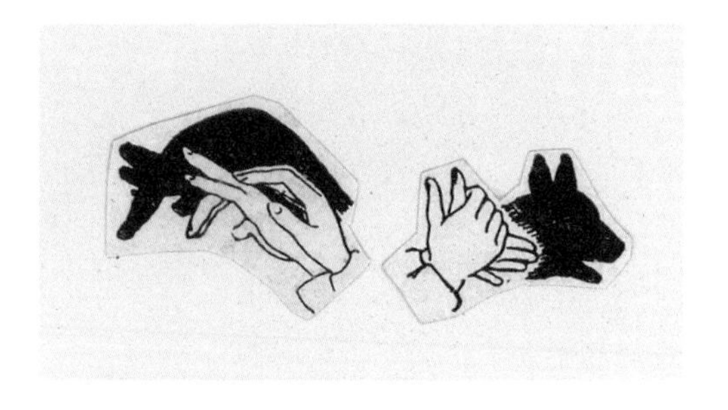

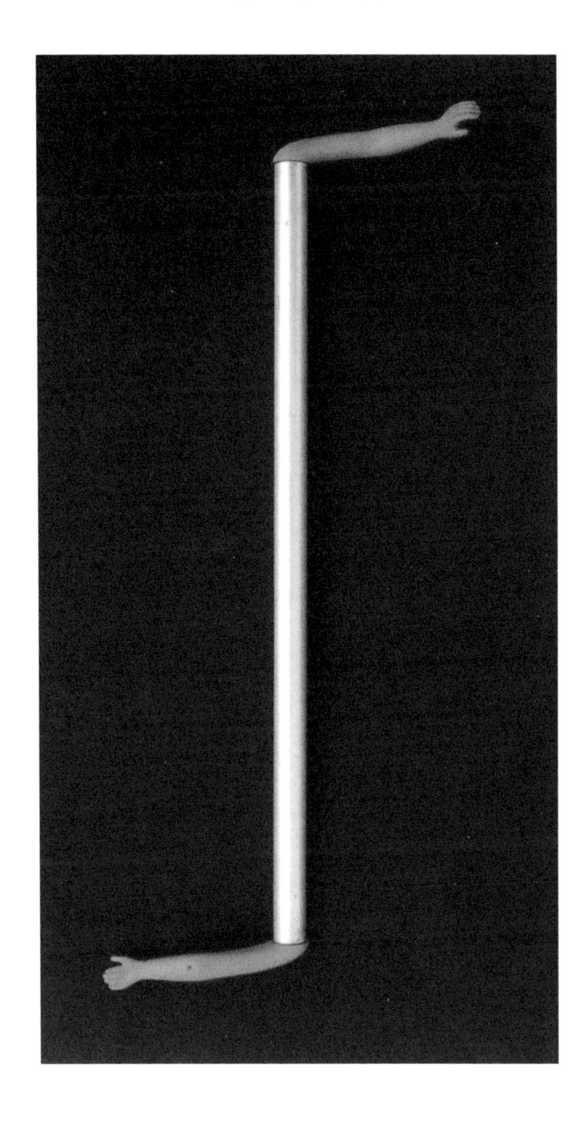

A fairy wand shaped like a scythe and employed to propel criminal fairies into the past or the future, according to the nature of their crime. This must be an ancient wand, because after inventing humans and watching them for a while, fairies soon became highly civilised and had no further need for such wands.

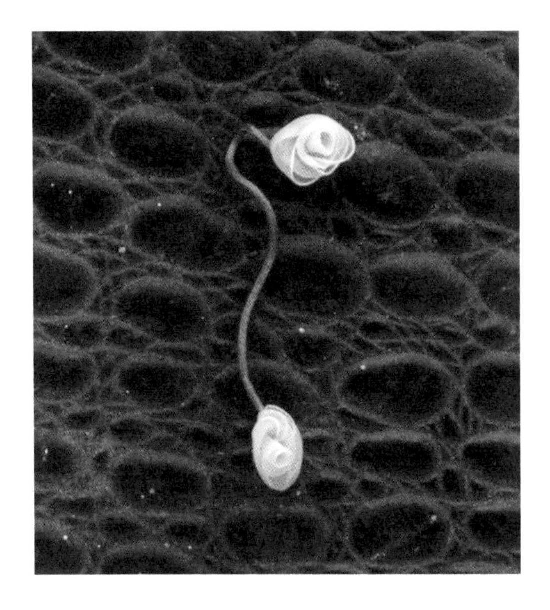

Known as 'The Eye Opener', this is one of several wands assembled by fairies from discarded human artefacts. Though not wielded as wands by the fairies, they obviously served as talismans or totems, or possibly as articles of ridicule which served to remind them of the errors of human ways. This wand seems to say that 'from the heart of a flower to the pupil of an eye' all is plain to observe, yet in sleeping and in blinking humans miss the half of it.

Fairies of course neither sleep nor blink. Each night they file into our heads to jumble any insights we may have stumbled on regarding the nature of existence. When the lights go out and silence falls, our very creators leap onto waiting dodgems inside our heads for the night ride.

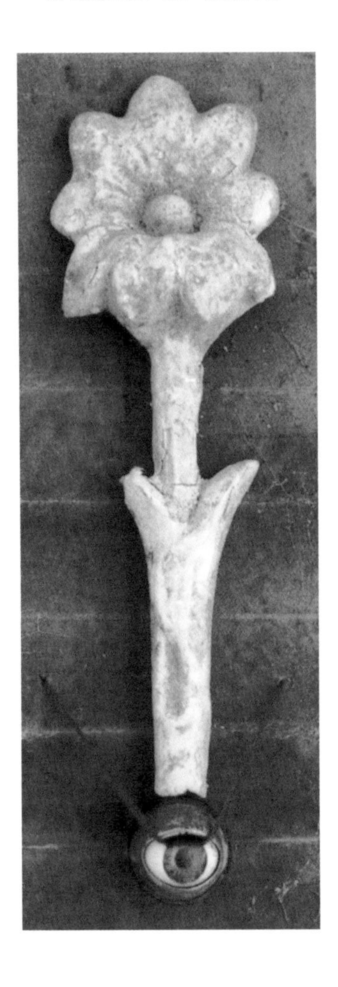

This 'typewriter key/aeroplane' wand may relate to the fairy invention of UFOs, tiny objects (e.g. bits of fluff) which fairies swoosh about rapidly a few inches in front of our faces, but which appear to be in focus only when we focus on infinity. This makes us believe they are far off, big and quick. This is an optical trick whose secret fairies have succeeded in keeping to themselves for a very long time.

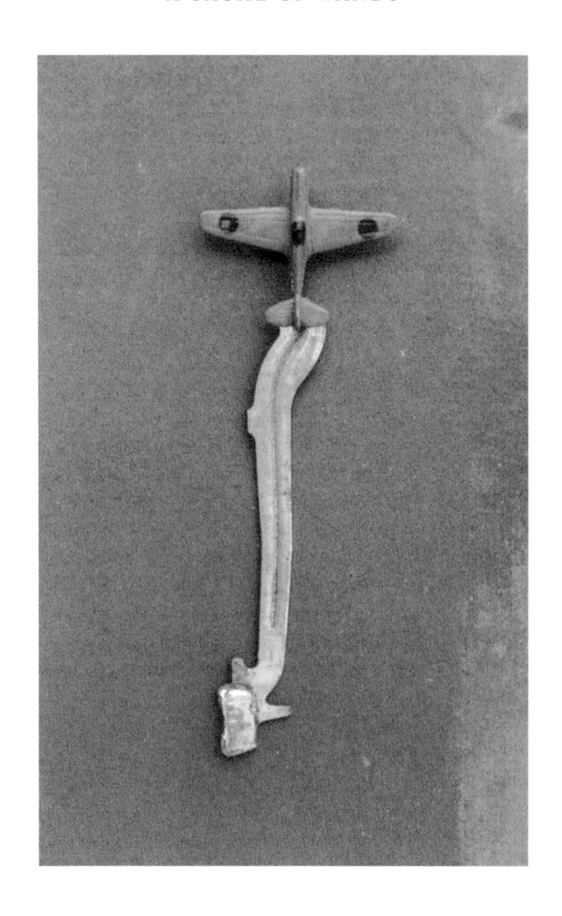

Here the human condition is represented by Punch and Judy, as victims of that original dilemma created by fairies when they fashioned us in separate halves. The *bottleur* brandishes his wand, a stick to tap and point, a relative of all pointers, staffs, rods, brushes, quills, batons and gavels.

But not only have we been divided in half: here the same face has a fixed expression but is viewed in different lights. As the sun moves on its daily course, fairies have ensured that it revolves a 'wheel of feelings' inside each human head. Tethered to the constellations, individuals must suffer continual change, thus remaining incapable of marshalling their thoughts or of clearly directing their actions.

Wise *Morose*

Attentive

Depressed *Ecstatic (drunk)*

This wand refers to the power fairies have over us because of language, which obscures so many simple truths. We cast our letters in lead to spell words and then these words cast us under their spell.

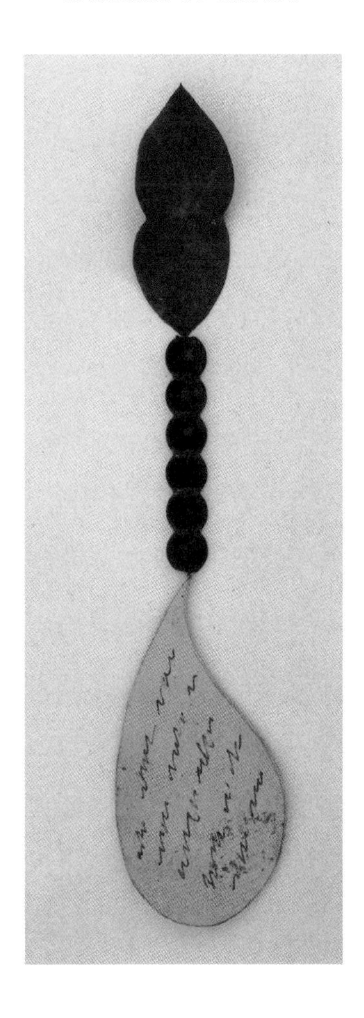

Three wands discovered together. The top wand is light. The middle one, however, is heavy. Made of lead, it could only have been wielded by the heftiest of fairies. The divided wand introduces a recurring theme of something split at one end (a wishbone is frequently used) with a pointer at the other. Fairies associate themselves with the former, humans with the latter, considering themselves to be broad-minded and humans narrow-minded.

A CACHE OF WANDS

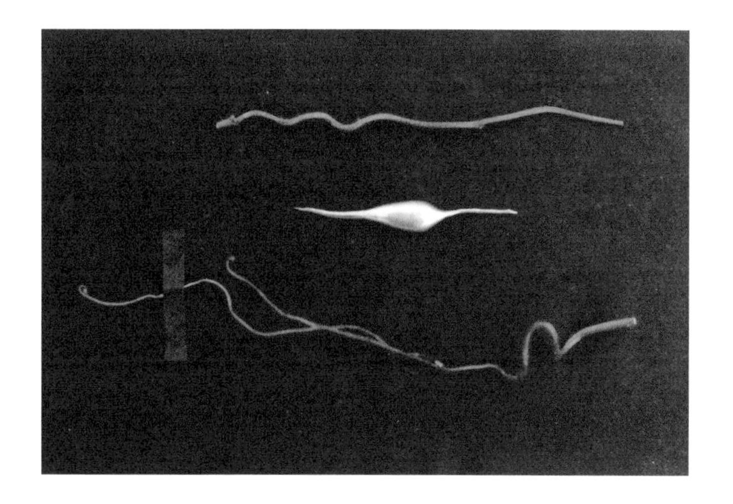

Pushed at night, we are steered in the dream state to become every nightmare that fairies wish to avoid, every foul deed. It is our misconduct that enables fairies to achieve perpetual nirvana. If fairies are at one end of an unbendable wand, we are tethered to the other.

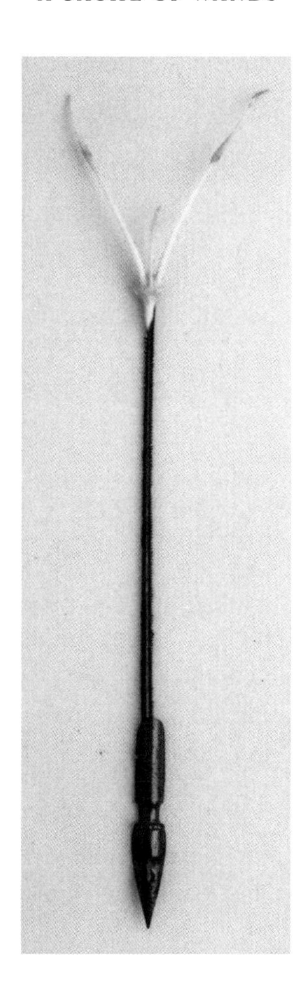

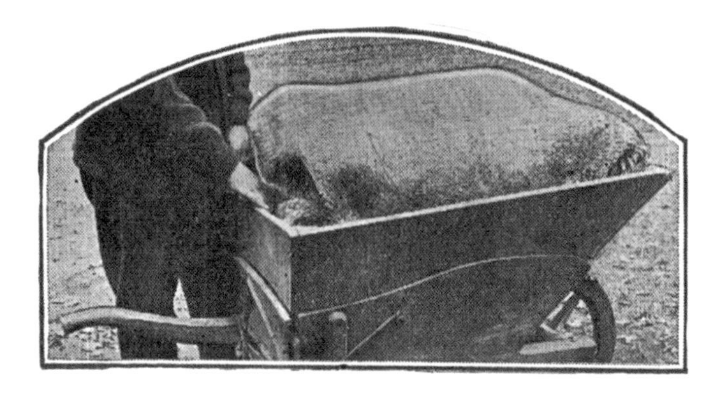

THE DREAM MIDWIVES

Five fairies (all right, four and a half)

Because humans were once cloned from fairies, we still retain faint traces of fairy memory. Wings for instance are something that we continue to feel the need for, though they have been transformed long since into shields to protect us (see soldiers on previous page) or large notepads.

Once, probably desperate to jot down something that he might otherwise have forgotten, a fairy wrote on the nearest thing to hand: his wing, which he then tore off and pocketed. (Writing may well have evolved from the intricate black veins on translucent wings.)

Although fairies moved beyond language and writing long ago, humans are still stuck with it, continuing to believe an awful lot of what they read, even though they know perfectly well it's all total bunkum.

The possibility of a mass-sighting at Bisley

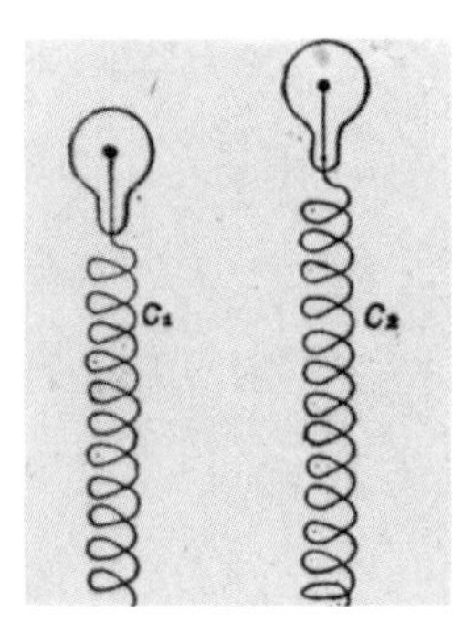

If C1 is taller than C2, C2 simply extends. Because they are unfixed, fairies are also easily able to alter their mental state.

When fairies first made humans they gave us 'belief' as a gift. But it was not really so much a gift to us as to themselves. It was if anything a handicap to us. But it is the wavering nature of our belief in fairies that keeps them fickle and unfixed. While some of us believe in them and some do not, others believe in them some of the time. It is this fluctuating characteristic of our belief that allows them to remain so changeable and to turn into something else instantly or to suddenly appear or disappear. These are things no other species can do and to do them fairies are entirely dependent on the human propensity to believe. In order that fairies can keep this essential human trait at the correct level of variance (slightly either side of a midpoint between extremes) a number of sentry fairies are given the responsibility of watching us and assessing the existing state of belief and adjusting it, for example with mass-sightings of fairies, or solitary glimpses . . .

rears with
up.
Circus

Fairies particularly enjoy the reactions of horses to a glimpse of them, preferably at the Derby or the Grand National.

Reports coming in of a fairy sighting in the Rockies and of another in London

If you look very closely at Shakespeare, Arthur Rackham, Gilbert and Sullivan or Sir James Barrie, you will notice they are made up out of lots and lots of little dots. Of course these are not really dots, but fairies. Each dot is a single fairy who has volunteered to form 'Sir James Barrie', etc, merely in order to boost a flagging belief in fairies in the sixteenth century or in 1904 or whenever.

SIR JAMES BARRIE

Humans will go to endless lengths for their beliefs. Some will even die for them. Here is a human searching for fairies in the Antarctic (and beginning to believe he might have got the wrong pole). This sort of dedication causes fairies a little wonder, though not the slightest desire to share in such obstinacy.

Fairies are not only particularly good at pretending to be dots, they can also do arrows. Arrows, like fairies, began on a serious note, associating themselves with function, survival and so on. But with the invention of humans (especially in their present state of perfection) fairies have grown by contrast (by contrast, that is, with their earlier selves as well as with humans) positively skittish.

400 BIOLOGY FOR TODAY

time in starting to do your studying or your work at home. First, you must decide that you want to break this habit. You must analyze the actions you now perform which take too long or which prevent your getting to work at once. When you have decided what new acts you want to perform and what old ones you want to eliminate, you begin your work vigorously, being careful to perform the acts you have planned and to leave out all that do not help. Whenever you have such tasks to perform, you follow your new plan without any exceptions. Before long you will have formed the new habit. You will then do your work without thinking much about the way in which you do it. In other words, the higher centers of the cerebrum will no longer be concerned with carrying out the new actions. The lower brain centers will take care of the habit automatically. If, however, during the formation of the habit you permit yourself to go back to the old habit of wasting time, the new habit will require much longer to establish. If you permit too frequent exceptions to the actions necessary in establishing the new habit, you will not succeed in forming it at all.

Fig. 262. Can you state some of the steps necessary in learning to play golf?

Continued learning. In the learning experiment with starfish described in an earlier part of this chapter, the biologist Jennings found that young starfish acquired the modified reflex more readily than did older specimens. Animal-trainers usually use young animals rather than old ones. Children often gain skill in games and other muscular activities more readily than do grown people. From observations such as these the old saying "You can't teach an old dog new tricks" has come to be widely accepted as applying

LEARNED RESPONSES 401

to all sorts of learning. It is often true that older people have more difficulty than children in learning to perform such muscular activities as those involved in playing the piano or in playing tennis. The greater difficulty, however, is probably not due to its being harder for them to learn but rather to changes in their bodies, or to the fact that usually they do not practice so faithfully or try so hard.

Whether one learns to play a game expertly or to perform intellectual tasks well depends largely upon how strongly one wants to succeed. "Old dogs" usually learn less easily than "young dogs" probably because they have less abundant energy; because they have undergone changes in bone and muscle; because they have no real desire to learn that particular skill; and possibly because they already have acquired habits which interfere with the new learning and which are difficult to break. Many experiments have shown that it is not true that children gain intellectual knowledge more rapidly than do older people. The contrary may even be the case. We gain new knowledge which involves the higher nerve centers of the cerebrum, such as learning to read a new language or to use higher mathematics, most easily in the early twenties. But there is so slight a loss of mental vigor as one gets older that, if one remains well and normal, there is no time of life when one cannot undertake new intellectual tasks with success.

Individual differences. If you have observed animals, you have no doubt noticed that some seem more intelligent than others. Jennings found that some of his starfish learned to turn over with one certain arm more readily than did others. In nature those animals of any kind which are the more "intelligent" — that is, the more able to learn quickly and effectively — are the ones most likely to grow to maturity and have offspring. Hence under natural conditions the "stupider" ones are likely to be eliminated by enemies, while the "brightest" and therefore the "fittest" are likely to survive.

Many people think that a person who is superior in one respect is likely to be very inferior in other respects. The opposite is the case. Though there are exceptions, it is in general true that the person who can do one sort of intellectual task well is likely also to be able to do other sorts of intellectual tasks well.

While the little girl is telling us important things about our world, a lot of fairies camouflaged as an arrow are directing our attention to her index finger, thereby alerting us to completely irrelevant issues such as the effect on the Pacific Ocean of her left arm. This smacks so much more of fairies than it does of earnest, helpful arrows.

Disguised as arrows, fairies will point at something (anything) in order to shift the emphasis, thus destroying any attempt at clarity made by real arrows.

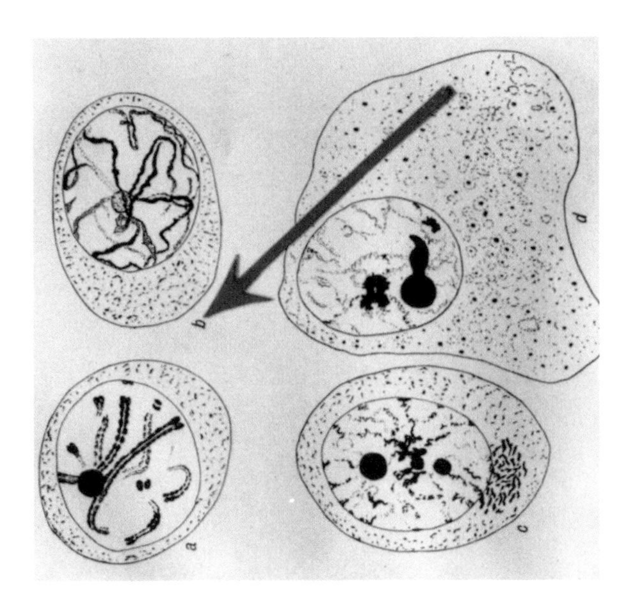
b
d
a
c

Fairies cannot resist taking risks. Creating humans so very like themselves was probably the biggest gamble they collectively ever made. But fairies built a number of safeguards into us, particular traits (handicaps) which would protect them. So we were doomed to remain a move or two behind our makers from the start.

Fairies decided we should be kept busy, in order that we should not find the time to think too deeply. And they came up with two wonderful time-wasters: eating and sleeping. The two fairies who patented these inventions made a mint. Not only did they patent sleep but cocoa, apple-pie beds and mattresses. They even patented falling asleep, tossing and turning while being unable to sleep and the whole fiasco of getting up in the morning and then falling down the stairs.

Sanding the upstairs landing (also patented)

But perhaps it was the capture and preparation of food, as well as its bottling and digestion, that really took the biscuit, though actually eating the food took very little time at all (to the continual chagrin of all those who must continually prepare it).

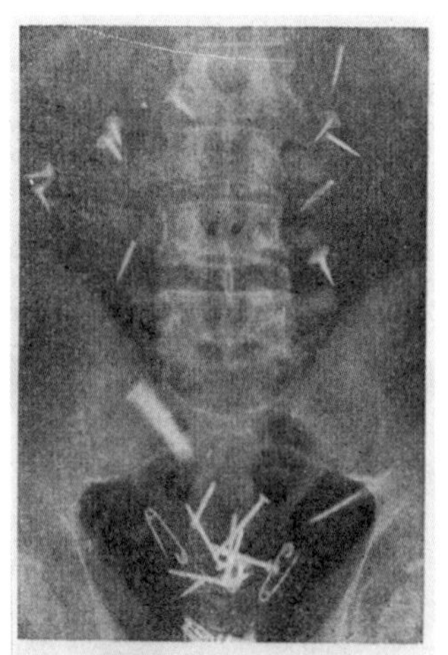

REVEALING X-RAYS
Left, penetrating the man's body from behind, X-rays throw shadows of bones and organs on to a screen. Above, the shadow picture (radiograph) reveals safety pins, nails and tacks swallowed by a child.

A lot of internal apparatus is also required to process the huge variety of stuff shovelled down humans, from bulky and completely useless substances like old teddy bears to highly dangerous or downright poisonous ones like tapioca and cabbage. And all these complex tubes, filters, juices and muscles, spasming to evacuate dolls' eyes, take up quite a lot of room and make us heavy and slow us down. We also spend a good deal of energy chasing meat and then surrounding ourselves with castles to digest it in. Another 'gift' fairies came up with was 'jealousy' . . .

Fairies invented jealousy because it is a very effective generator of hatred, which causes wars, which takes up more time *and* provides fairies with great entertainment (as well as something to bet on). But this hatred has another benefit. By making people move away from one another, it forces them into much colder regions so that they waste even more time manufacturing galoshes and ironing.

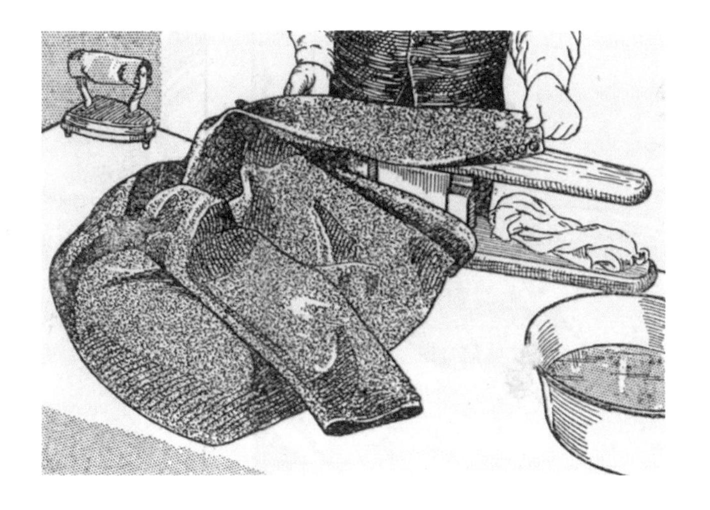

Though fairies have no need of teeth, they will often put some in, just to wear them out. Many fairies do a roaring trade in dentures. But real teeth are another matter. As we know, in order to be initiated into full fairyhood, each fairy youth first has to seize a human tooth. The ivory from human milk teeth is highly prized and worked by them into crudely made little guns, with which they pretend to shoot one another.

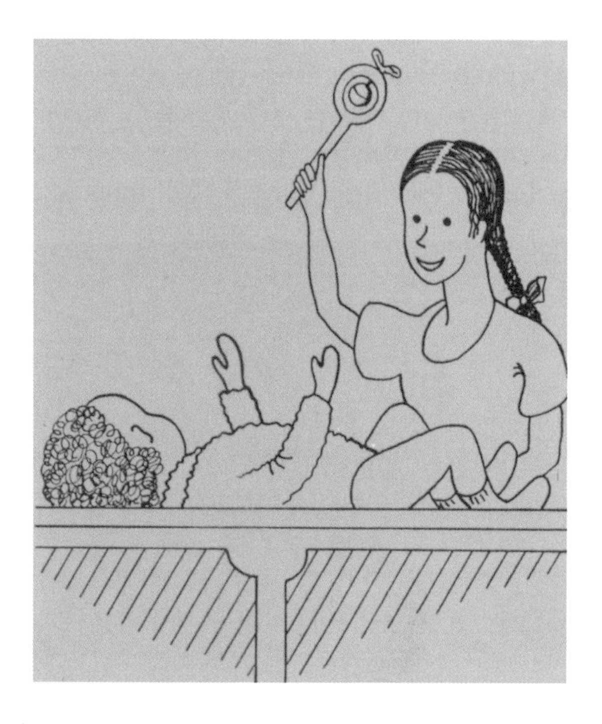

A fairy disguised as a girl, about to knock out a baby's tooth with its own rattle

A fairy disguised as Freud selecting a choice tooth while distracting his victim by wobbling flowers

Fairies are like anything that looks lovely at first,
but as soon as you pry or dig a little . . .

As we have learned, fairies love to ape all human activities. Mock battles are extremely popular, with fairies being winched onto horses or strapped into aeroplanes made of lead. Sieges last for days, with hundreds of fairies holed up in a box of live matches. The end result is always far more fairies than they started with, because they all laugh so much.

Fairy TV is full of clever skits about human behaviour and fairy films are heavily into satire and black humour, especially the genre known as . . .

'FILMS ON COAL'

A great deal of fun is had by fairies pretending to make films. For example, a fairy director will get up very early and spend hours in make-up, before bossing all the other fairies around in front of and behind the pretend camera. Because he does this so earnestly and with such ruthlessness they all laugh for days and days, causing yet another surge in the fairy population.

167

'Cut. You looked in the camera yet again.
Take 168 had better be the last . . .'

The fairy director, the one in the wings, explains:
'She gives you the glass, then *you drink from it, you nit.'*

'That was just awful. Here, try it on this.'

'You read him this piece here, then just as you finish he bites your leg off. You yell loudly as he runs off with it, scaring the boatman who tips his passengers into the river where they are all swallowed by sharks.'

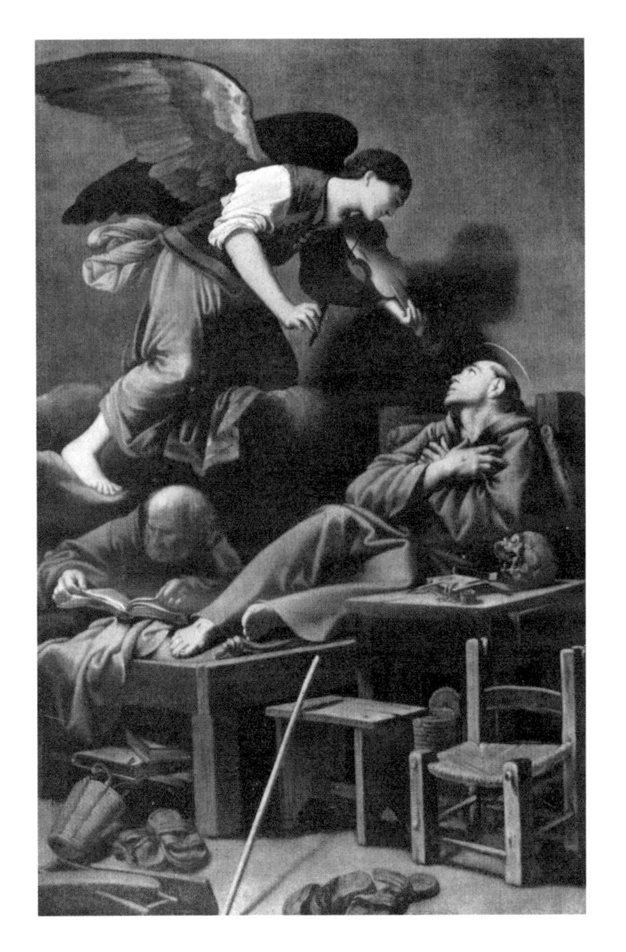

Director (under his breath): 'This time you've got a prompt and I've set you in the mood. If you get it wrong again I'll, I'll . . .'

A fairy about to do shrinking . . .

The outcome of most fairy activities results in laughter and consequently huge increases in the fairy population are very common. Since fairies do not die, there could well be a problem. Surely the little folk will crowd out all the other species? No, there is plenty of room, for fairies can easily adjust their size, right down to the subatomic level.

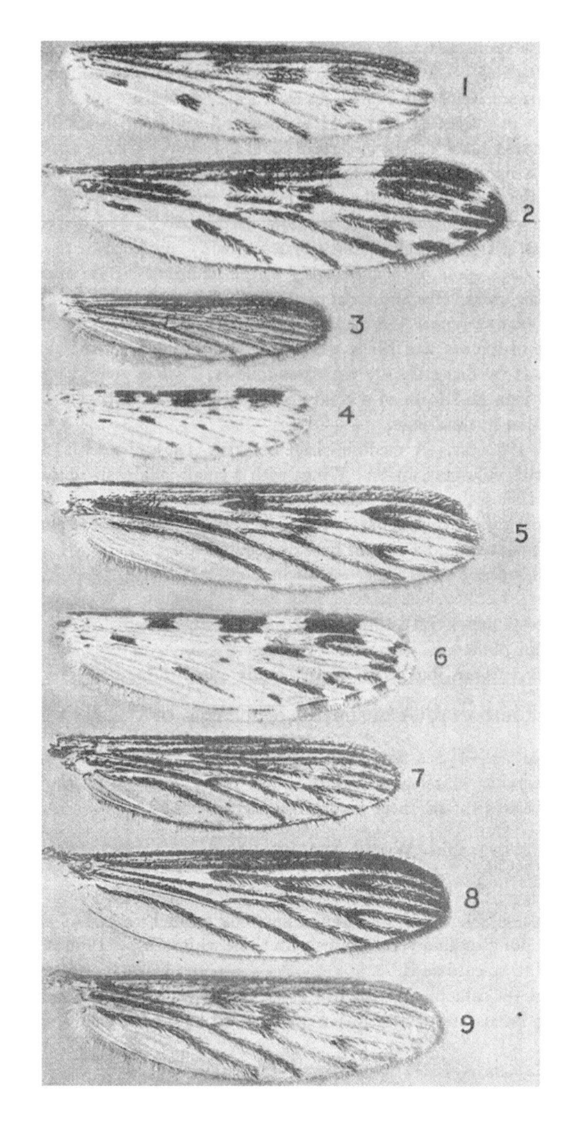
1
2
3
4
5
6
7
8
9

The fairy attitude to humans is that they consider us to be firstly their laboratory rats and secondly a long-running comedy act. They do not think that this is at all unfair. They have no concept of right or wrong because they do not have any language. Fairies tried language but only for about ten minutes. That's how long it took them to see right through it.

Opposite: We can only guess at what the ancient fairy language might have been able to convey. The spots and stripes on fairy wings seem to represent some sort of code, though nowadays they probably only serve a decorative function. A breakthrough in decoding these patterns was made a few years ago when a human code-breaker noticed certain key 'words' recurring again and again, like 'power boat'.

Laughter is all and everything to fairies and the many varieties of laughter provide them with a great enough range of expression to last until eternity. On the rare occasion when a fairy runs out of material it only needs to observe humans.

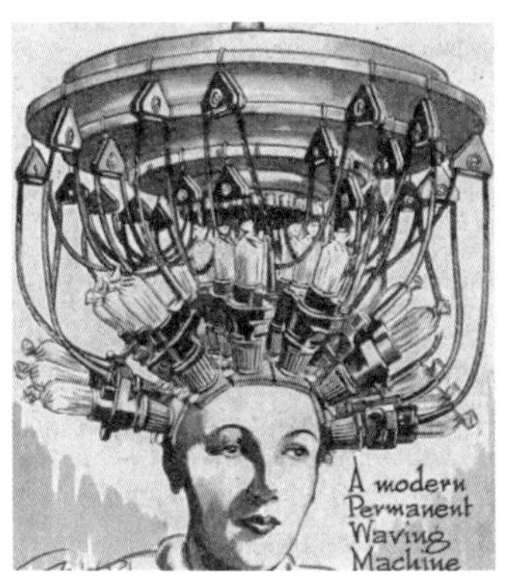

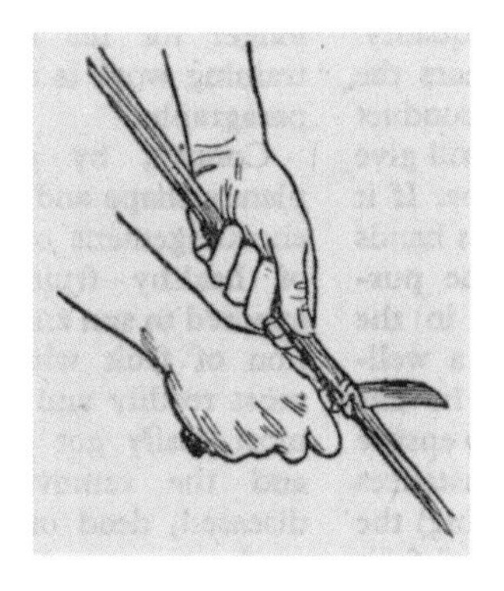

When fairies watch humans, they cannot fail to notice that there are some who exhibit certain traits similar to those displayed by fairies . . .

. . . like being infuriating.

And they wondered why the coffee hadn't tasted quite as good as usual.

Historically this may be the most infuriating and premeditatedly callous thing any human or fairy can do to another during peacetime (also known as 'pax') – tapping another's ball completely off the lawn.

An infuriating fairy off to the left has probably just said something infuriating.

One fairy is stealing another's soup through a straw. See if you can guess which one is infuriating.

An infuriating female fairy giving two male fairies false directions (to the Carlton Club).

Whereas a few humans are occasionally infuriating, most fairies are infuriating quite a lot of the time. For instance when you are out at night watching for meteors the infuriating fairy is the one who shouts 'Wah – what a beauty' when it hasn't really seen one at all. When all the other fairies look around, the infuriating fairy says 'Wow, another', pointing to where the others were all just looking. There is no doubt that this is an infuriating fairy.

One fairy looking down at another and telling him he's going up *the 'down' stairs.*

Actually, it's for Gerald, and he's twelve.

Several fairies forcing pilgrims right back to where they started, just when they had nearly got to where they were going.

A fairy about to pretend she is infuriated at being fooled into believing that she's won a holiday for two to the Fens by 2,000 fairies pretending to be a telephone.

A fairy supergluing another one's foot to a stool while several pairs of fairies rush about with lavatories, empties to the right, full ones to the left (must be a large function on the right).

Fairies get a lot of ideas from watching humans but it is our dreams that provide them with the greatest source of humour. Because fairies cannot dream, they fashioned us to make dreams for them. So it is we, therefore, who are the dream midwives.

Fairy levelling

THE FAIRY WARS

When a fairy is making love or war, cracking jokes or fleas, manufacturing raffia mats or anti-personnel mines, whether he or she is playing a tune or the fool, writing poetry or filling in o's, whatever it is, it's all posturing. Fairies are always only ever posturing.

Fairies imitating humans who are desperate to get away but pretending they've had a jolly good time while waving goodbye

Pretending to have writer's block (head in hands, big and little sighs) is an old favourite. Striking attitudes is what fairies are really best at. Though to them language is totally useless and meaningless, being a poet is great fun because it gives fairies new ways of holding their heads and limbs, the forlorn expressions, the inky fingers and so on. To fairies, books are just props and so are tables, reams of blank paper, inkwells, distant views, dictionaries, floors (for staring at), muses and all the other accoutrements and paraphernalia necessary for the production of poetry.

Mr Henry Welby. Gt
Ætatis Suæ 84

Fairies get a lot of fun out of pretending to be humans but they have also learned a thing or two from them, like 'changing one's mind'. The greatest stride forward in fairy evolution as a species might well be attributed to this mental breakthrough, this mutability, observed by them in the human species. Indeed, the physical equivalent of changing one's mind, which is 'changing direction', has become one of the main fairy characteristics. To those who have to live with it it can be infuriating. But it is endearing to those who just drop in to borrow a spear.

Porto Rico
Prevailing Westerlies
Horse Latitudes
TROPIC OF CANCER
Trades
"Doldrums" (Feeble Winds)

Fairies soon developed a facility for changing to any size. From the human point of view, the smaller a fairy is and the less of them there are, the more you need to start worrying. In groups, fairies are generally fine. But put one on its own and there's usually a mess to clear up. A nuclear fairy is a hell of a thing.

All fairies are very keen on hats. On average a fairy will have 2,000 hats. Because fairies normally downsize to go out, most of their hats are very small (this uses less material and saves storage). But the main reason for downsizing when fairies go out is it helps considerably with the car-sharing.

Since fairies do not eat, they love the whole idea of food and this picture of a pre-war German sausage factory near Wuppertal is typical of the sort of thing they take photographs of.

This is probably a genuine fairy photo because fakes are mostly taken by humans who, because they think fairies are small, take them from low down.

When fairies reach eleven, a switch is automatically triggered and from then on they pretend full-time, wearing their emotions like hats. For example if a fairy is cross it only lasts a moment because like any emotion, it isn't genuine. Because fairies are incapable of being serious, they never take themselves seriously. At fairy auctions for instance all the fairies always bid against one another for the fakes.

Take the dragon fairy in all the 'St George and' pictures. He's nearly always shown in a bad way, usually skewered. Remember though that the artist is paid by the bishop and bishops are very keen on saintly exterminators getting a good press, so the following moments are never portrayed, those during which the dragon grabs hold of the lance and hurls St George off the horse (because he doesn't think to let go of it and anyway he is trying hard to impress the lady and pose for the artist). But fairies don't really care and quite enjoy pretending to be bad.

Humans are always forgetting that fairies do not, cannot, die. Fighting to fairies is just a game. But if fighting only ever just led to internal bleeding, they probably wouldn't bother with it. Because war means wounds and scars, they love it to bits. It is in fact one of the main fairy occupations. Fairy campaigns have been known to go on as long as human ones. The difference is that fairies *want* to be wounded. They love pretending to be shot and because the whole thing is really about dressing up. During a siege for instance, they are constantly checking the state of their disarray in full-sized mirrors. Fairies do not have to be better armed than their opponents. In fact they go to endless lengths not to be, because being worse-equipped leads to far greater injuries. Dressing up is second in popularity to making up. This is not what fairies do after wars, it's what they do before the war starts and during it, many times. Fairies will spend hours in make-up before a battle. But the best thing about wars and the real reason why fairies invest so much time and energy in fighting (even more than in lovemaking), is because it allows them to constantly alter their make-up. To begin with there are bruises and contusions and superficial cuts, followed by burns and minor wounds, followed by deep wounds, scars and gammy legs. There are also endless excuses to do moaning and thrashing about and moving around with shellshock or with arrows sticking out. The whole object of a fairy war is to get thoroughly wounded, as many times as possible. The competition is not to overcome one's foe but to manoeuvre oneself carefully into a position of weakness, so one can be taken completely by surprise and vanquished. Fairies love being vanquished. On the eve of battle, fairies draw lots and the losers get the big guns, the aircraft carriers and the tanks whereas the winners get pebbles.

'Your hat's a bit crooked.'

It has been pointed out earlier that fairies do not die. So when they are fighting, where the blades go is of little consequence. Other things, though, like the angle of a hat, are really very critical.

A fairy archer about to slip over on his arrows accidentally on purpose

All fairies prefer fluffy bullets because then there is plenty of time to get in their way. A fairy who has got successfully in the direct line of a fluffy bullet will try out their latest death roll, which they will have been practising for days in front of one of the large mirrors wheeled to the front by thousands of fairy mirror-bearers.

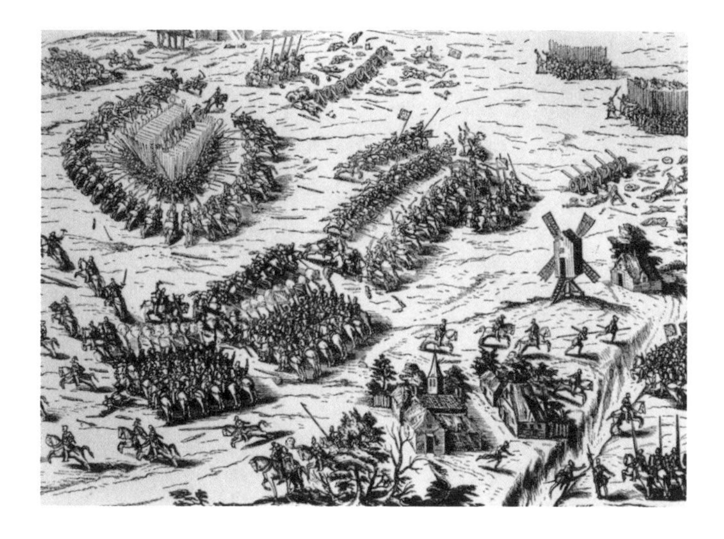

A platoon of fairy pike-bearers with their pikes upright will turn suddenly, moving along like a hairbrush. The execution of such swift changes of speed and direction, at which fairies excel, is truly marvellous. Though starlings are quick, they have nothing on fairies. And anyway, when starlings try it with pikes they get in a hell of a mess.

Fairy airforce. Also known as fairyforce.

Four real fairies followed by a lot of shadows. Over the centuries fairies have perfected the art of indefinite repetition. After all, they've had little better to do. Using the technique, a single line of fairies can quickly turn into a whole brigade, then a division.

A fairy thinking. No leap of the imagination is required by an observer since such an observer does not have to take it on trust that this fairy is thinking just because someone says they are, because here the thinking part is actually sewn onto the hat.

Things one cannot see any evidence of, things that require an element of trust, like being shown some very neat invisible mending, such things are of no interest to fairies. In fact they are anathema to them. Fairies are not interested in subtleties, especially if they have to be taken on trust. What they like is the maximum effect for the minimum effort.

Here fairy cavalry is doing the indefinite repetition thing, but this time they are doing it by moving backwards.

It is useful if we wish to understand more about fairies (and of course we are well aware that there are plenty who do not), to take a look at how their wings evolved. We know that at some stage in their evolution, these flaps became detachable, then optional, until finally they were just worn on special occasions (e.g. beheadings).

'Arise Sir Fairy Knight of the detachable wing which we can't see because it's folded inside your hat.'

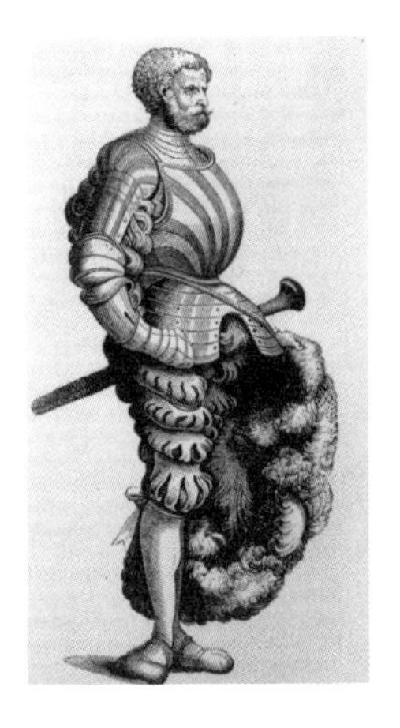

Warm removable wing

Small but handy detachable wing

Fairy wing converted into a quill. This is not easy to write with in a wind. This fairy is having difficulties and has just written all over herself.

Note how these wings are folded up into frilly bits on the shoulders which jiggle about as the fairy soldiers bounce along.

Handy camping wings

Horn-hiding hoods. The one on the right has been caught without her hood on.

Because our own evolution is rather more closely associated with fairies than we would be happy to admit (they begat us), this wing thing is intrinsic. It has been suggested by a fairy psychologist that the human love of (obsession with) symmetry relates to having once had wings ourselves and then having suddenly lost them, both at once. To compensate for the loss we are still forever arranging things neatly, symmetrically.

Example of the human love of symmetry
(shame about the shadows though)

1. This portrait was taken solely by the light of two ordinary matches seen in the picture.

Of course they are not ordinary matches. She believes they are (she believes in matches), but in fact they are fairies beating their wings very rapidly together to create fake light. Once again, observe the wing reference and symmetry.

Symmetrical boxers. When fairies box it has nothing to do with winning or wounding. It's all choreography, parody and terminology. Points are awarded for symmetrical arrangements, which fairies find so difficult to achieve.

Here four fairies appear very positive and symmetrical one moment and then positively negative and indecisive the next.

Humans frequently blame fairies for such pixilated activities as this and will even, in extreme circumstances, for instance when no doors have been forced, no windows broken, accuse the little folk of burglary, refusing to entertain the idea that it might have been an 'inside job'. Here the careful arrangement of the drawers, the incredibly controlled disorder, is a dead giveaway, betraying obvious human symmetrical precision, of which fairies are practically incapable.

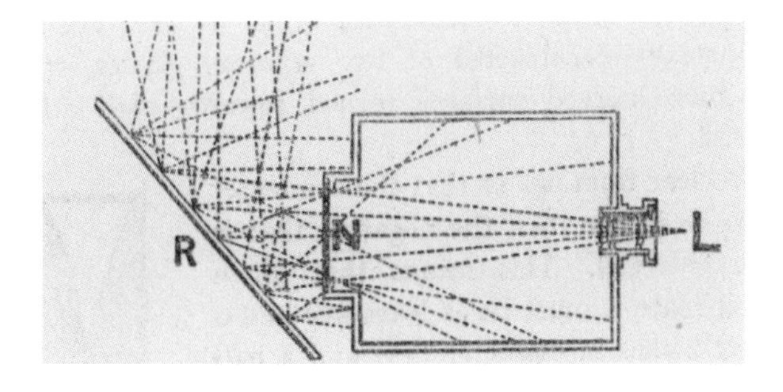

Fairies have a strong disinclination towards symmetry. The above is an example of their love of confusion, taking something that is really quite straightforward and making a real mess of it.

Humans have not got anything on fairies when it comes to complexity. Just take a look at a little of what lies behind one small ordinary fairy light.

While at an early age humans learn to use numbers (most humans, there are exceptions), fairies employ strips of paper instead of tape measures and rulers. The world to them is far more fun if it is approximate.

Whereas humans generally try to solve problems, fairies enjoy being the problem. Here are some fairies being a problem, pretending to be fruit.

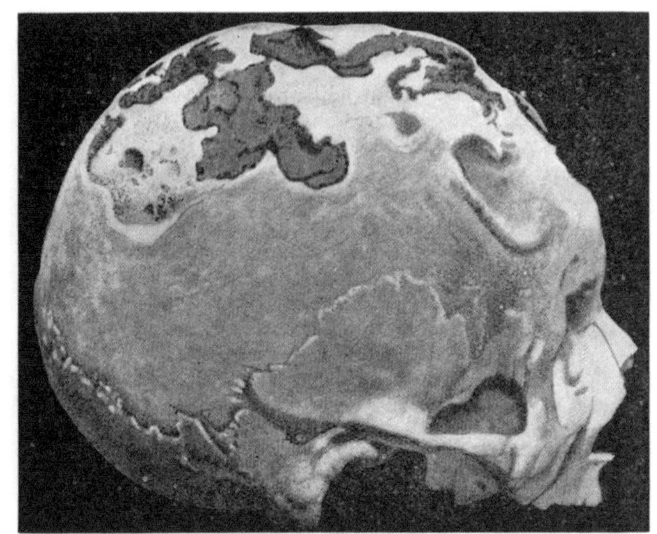

Courtesy [" *Practice of Surgery,*" *Spencer and Gask* (*J. & A. Churchill*

Humans obviously hope to turn the whole world into a human skull. Fairies just have to laugh at us for believing that we were created in order to inherit the earth. Fairies (our makers) never had any intention of giving it to us or even of growing old themselves, let alone of dying or making a will or anything. This whole thorny question of the creation of humans has never been tackled more firmly nor explained more lucidly than by the eminent fairy evolutionist who has put it all in a nutshell. 'They didn't dream us up, we built them – out of some old bones we found in a pit . . .'

One day an assistant came up with an idea for breasts.

Having just created the first human being (well, not quite 'being' yet), four fairies are actually cupping butterflies in their hands. Anyone looking at them would think they are about to imbue those dry old bones with life. But really they just like the tickly feel.

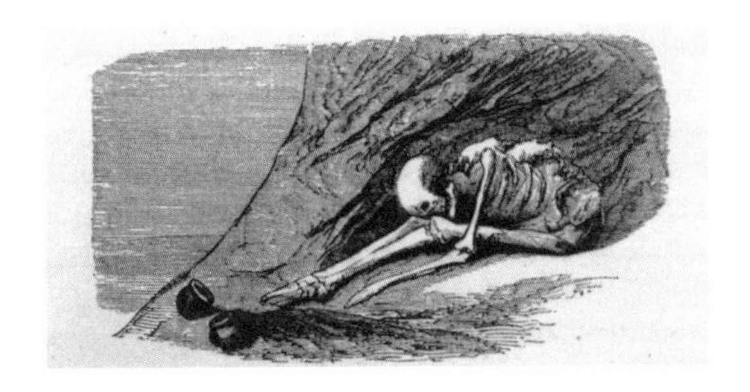

'Death of a prophet', a scene arranged carefully by fairies so that when filmed coming to life (in the propagation room) and then projected backwards, it will look as if he's starving to death because he can't quite reach his porridge.

A fairy sketch to explain to new fairies (or old fairies at evening classes) what goes on in the propagation room.

Teaching is simply another excuse for adopting attitudes. All fairies know that being taught anything at all is a total waste of time.

There are a few freak fairies who mumble and pontificate about the creation of the first fairies while pointing with sticks at diagrams and apparently making things crystal clear when everyone knows they are as murky as heck. But any fairies watching get a lot of laughs out of the antics of these fairy know-it-alls. Fairies also laugh a lot at our beliefs. But really they are a little more like us than we would care to admit. Fairies may not talk, eat, sleep or die, but we believe they are missing an opportunity for we derive a lot of pleasure from sleeping, eating, talking, debating, arguing and killing one another.

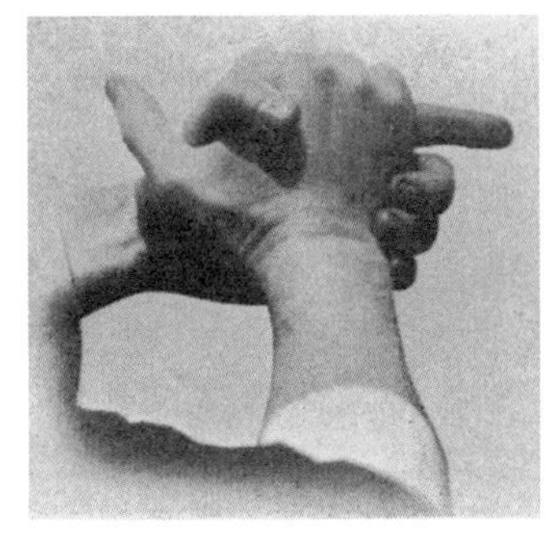

Fairies get many of their ideas for new species simply by throwing shadows on their burrow walls.

When fairies feel the need for a new species, they just glue some old bones together with something a bit tacky (not very tacky and certainly not quick-set or impact) because they like to be able to backtrack whenever they get a much funnier idea. Then when they shut the propagation room door and let in the single-cell organisms through a tiny hatch, these rush in and invade the bony structure, quickly becoming all its working parts. Our idea of Eden was really the propagation room when the fairy scientist entered it early one morning forgetting he'd started some creatures off the night before and that he'd made them in his own image and thinking it was just a couple of his own assistants messing about. So he told them to get out. Well, he pointed and they got the message.

GENESIS.
Chap. III, V. 6.
Mans shameful fall

And of course in human terms we have suffered a lot ever since, blaming bad apples, good apples, any old apples, snakes, gods, gardens, worms, tadpoles, trees, shrubs, hedges, water lilies and peonies, but especially each other, for everything whenever it goes wrong. Probably if there was nothing to blame, nothing would go wrong. As a fairy anthropologist once remarked to his class: 'If there was nothing and no one to blame, humans would make sure nothing went wrong. But having built into them this "It'll all go wrong" thing, guess what, it all goes wrong . . .'

Fig. 5.

A fairy pretending to kill itself. Fairies will pretend to eat or drink absolutely anything. They just do not die.

FIG. 153.—Action of Sulphuric Acid on Sugar.

And this of course is what fairies want. The more we go wrong the better the example of awfulness we provide them with. Imagine you are a little brother and your big sister is naughty and gets told off. What happens? Yes, you smirk. Fairies have spent hundreds of thousands of years perfecting smirking. When it comes to smirking we have a long way to go. Fairies would lose an awful lot to laugh at if we stopped doing things badly and blaming one another and arranging ornaments tidily on shelves and blowing each other to smithereens.

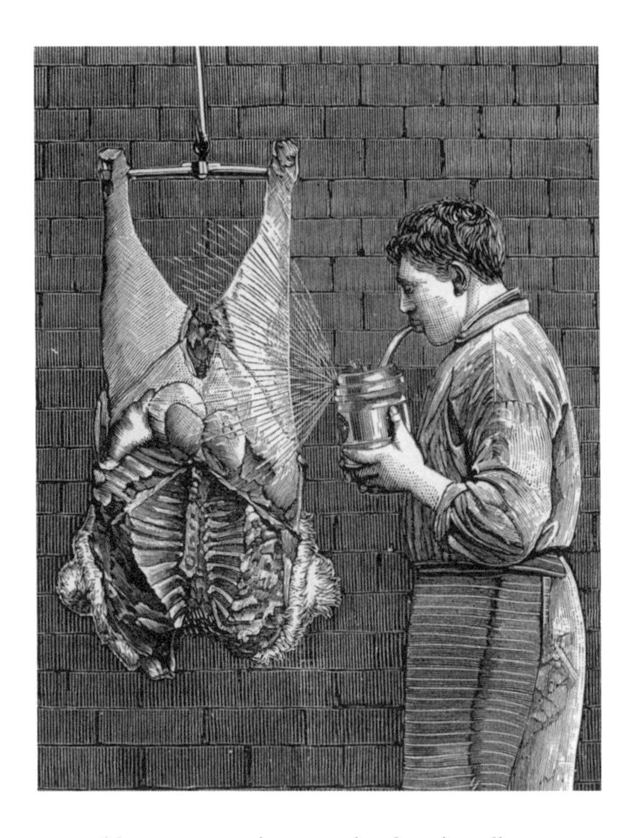

A human protecting an animal against disease

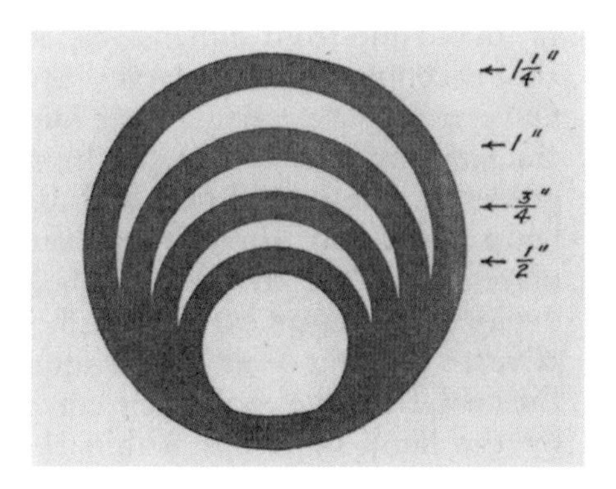

A fairy shrinking imperially

Because fairies can shrink easily, to the size of a virus if they want, they can put any human they want out of the way for a while – in bed with a cold, flu, pneumonia, bubonic plague and/or backache. Fairies love diseases because of the make-up, especially impetigo.

Although fairies are incredibly adaptable, they like to make out it's a lot of work – so they will go into bouts of pretend training, for example by pretend eating black-and-white food for days and days before appearing on black-and-white TV.

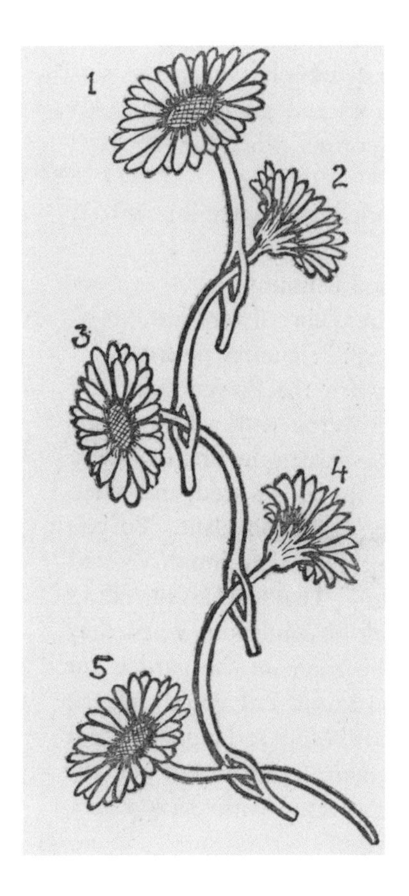

In fact fairies are so adaptable that they will even dress up to look like flowers, completely altering their usual sexual arrangements just to help out an unsuspecting fairy sociologist with her thesis on the antics of daisies.

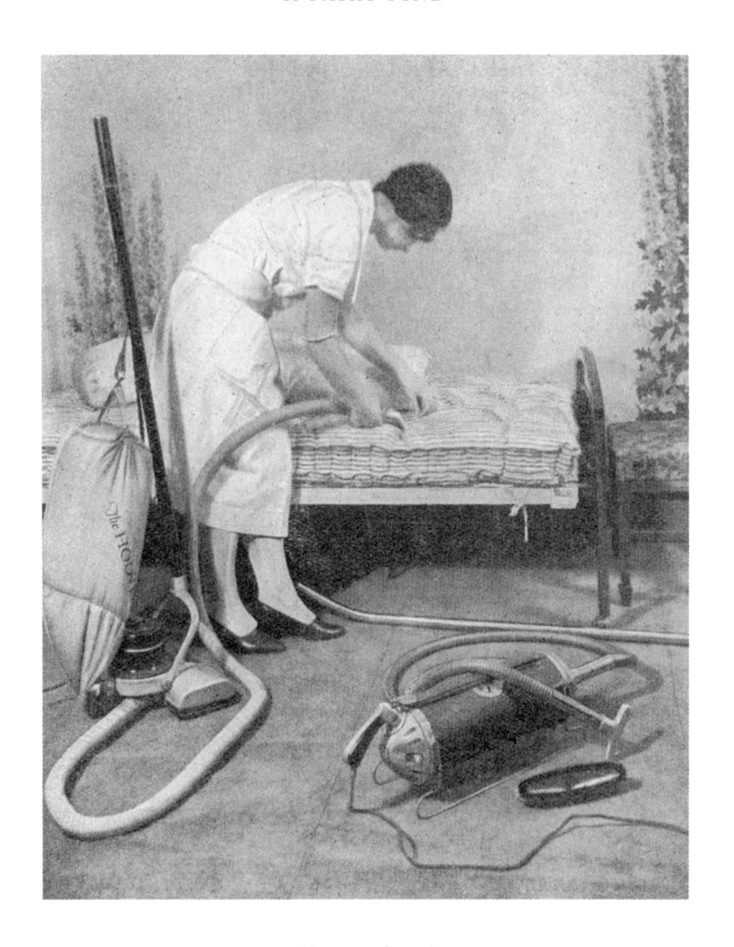

Human female

We will not go into the sexual antics of fairies here. Let us just say that they are every bit as inventive as humans when it comes to pleasure but at a much tenderer age. Humans discourage sex in their young because they might make babies. But fairies only do sex for fun. Nor do new fairies represent any threat to sleep or the family purse. They just pop out whole, don't eat, don't need high chairs, stair guards, rusks or nappies, they are recognised as being unteachable, don't require any clothing or need a cot to wet nor take up any extra space, because the others just downsize a micron to accommodate them. It is reckoned that one fairy will produce a million more and remember all their birthdays.

A corner of the propagation room. In fairy terms 'room' means a space. It is much more approximate and can include outdoors, if it wants.

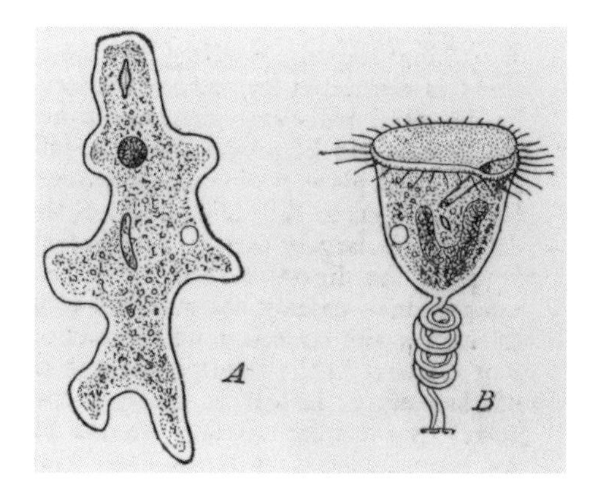

Our beginning had nothing to do with primordial soup or a cocktail of tiny organisms . . .

We now know that fairies created humans and we know roughly how they did it. It was not at a cellular level nor in any way an intensely focussed technical procedure, but a random hit-and-miss process that led to a lot of hilarity on the laboratory table, all of it at our expense.

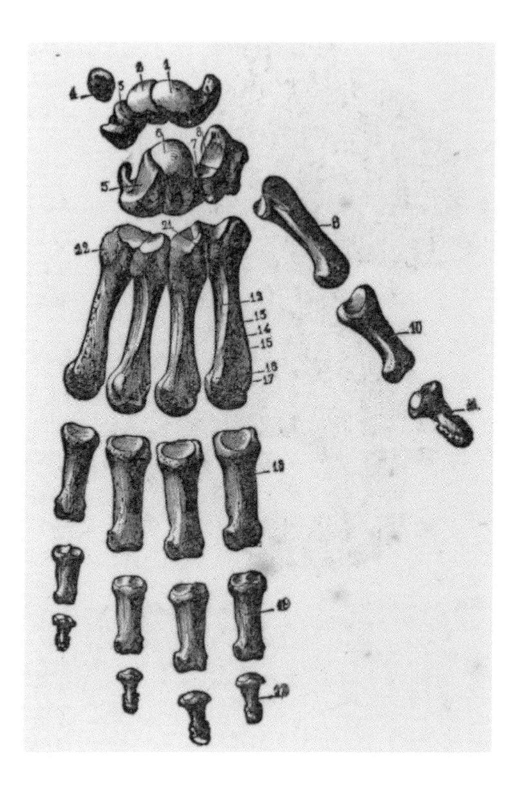

The process that led from the pile of stuff on the left to the thing above was not, as you might imagine, the result of a great leap of the imagination or even of anything painstaking. On the contrary . . .

Collapsible picker centre gumming for neck ring

Humans were achieved not with the sort of precision required to gum an awful lot of labels onto exactly the same number of bottles while all these are travelling ridiculously quickly. They were achieved instead with something approaching irresponsibility and with absolutely no concern whatsoever for the outcome.

The kind of drive or 'focus of attention' onto a single thing which leads humans to achieve so much in so many fields holds no interest whatsoever for fairies.

When playing ball games, fairies just whack the ball. There is no such thing as a common goal or team spirit, no sense of pulling together. It is just every fairy for himself.

At first glance this would appear to be two fairies doing press-ups, but of course since this is an impossible concept, it is just what it in fact is, which is onions doing them. Fairies have no interest in fitness nor any idea of doing anything together (except of course laughing and sex).

And of course it is entirely thanks to such wayward fairy characteristics that human kind was born. (The 'kind' bit was added later, by humans.)

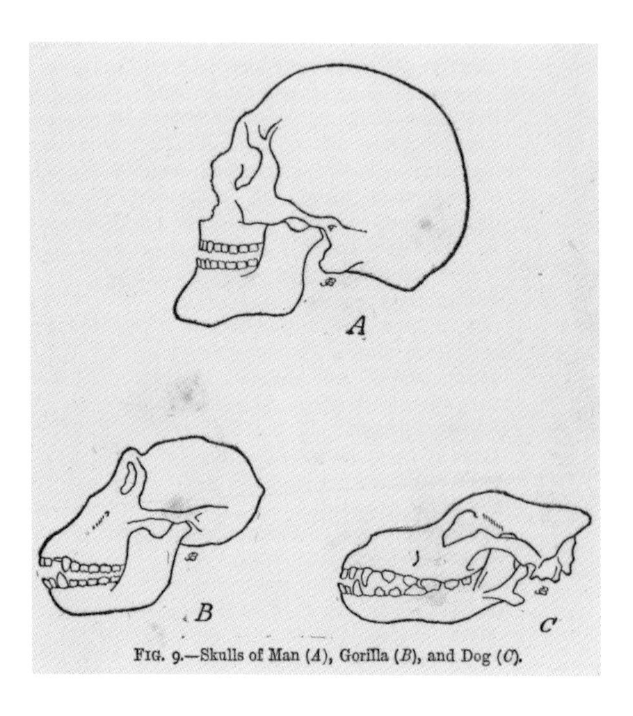

FIG. 9.—Skulls of Man (*A*), Gorilla (*B*), and Dog (*C*).

Although these skulls are from separate species, fairies created them in a few moments. They simply put C in a vacuum chamber for a bit and when they opened the door they had B, so they shut the door again and three seconds later they had A. Simple.

As we all know, fairies are male and female, back and front. So how they came up with split-sex humans is still an issue dogged by conjecture. One theory has it that a bone-room assistant was mucking about with some clay and left a figure overnight. The next day she found someone had cut it in half so she reported the violation. Her boss came to look and started laughing, twitching his features in a way that meant 'Tell you what, Titania (or Semolina or whatever), carry on along these lines. Your saboteur may have hit on something.' And so two humans, with only half a set of genitalia each, were let loose. And look what it led to: croquet, religion, jam tarts, trench warfare and indigo eye liner.

Which brings us back to fairy wars. As well as dressing up, applying make-up, large-scale choreography and disease, fairies love wars because of the laughter that breaks out when they are pretending to be serious and when one fairy does something even only slightly funny and a whole regiment collapses completely, falls on its swords and rolls around out of formation and . . . suddenly there's another whole regiment of new fairies. Many fairy wars begin with just two or three fairies and end up with thousands upon thousands.

Fairies find that the greater the discrepancies that exist between opponents, the more fun there is to be had and the more unexpected the outcome . . .

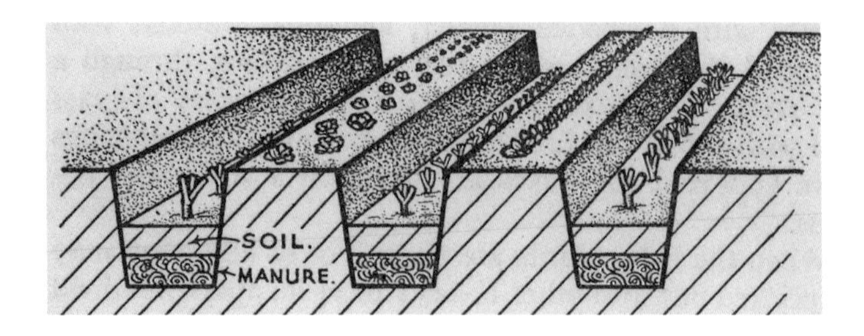

. . . for example, like this fairy-in-shining-armour who has just been run over by a Chieftain tank.

It is quite likely that humans and fairies are in perfect harmony, in the sense that everything is weighted heavily against humans (those are the humans on the right).

But who is this?

FIND OUT IN THE NEXT EXCITING VOLUME

A fairy taking fake human photographs

ACKNOWLEDGEMENTS

With thanks to John McDowall, Sheila Lanyon, Yvonne Lewer, Tanya Peixoto, Alan Healey and the Helston Community Centre, Jacqie Levin, Jo and Lil Lanyon, Sam Lanyon, Esmé Maylam, Rosa Levin, Bruno Martin, Markham Moore, Jane Turnbull, Jessica Mann, the London Institute of Pataphysics and all those involved in making the fairy films as well as the fairies themselves.

With thanks also to the following for permission to reproduce images:

The Archive of Modern Conflict, London. Cambridge University Press for *An Introduction to the Study of Cytology* by L. Doncaster, 1920. Elsevier for graphics reprinted from *The World of the Children*, in four volumes, by Stuart Miall, the Caxton Publishing Company Ltd., 1948. And by permission of the Estate of Stuart Miall. Koninklijk Museum voor Schone Kunsten, Antwerp, Belgium, for Jan Van Eyck's *Saint Barbara*. The Oriental Institute, University of Chicago, for photograph from *Archaeology from the Earth* by Sir Mortimer Wheeler, Penguin Books, 1956.

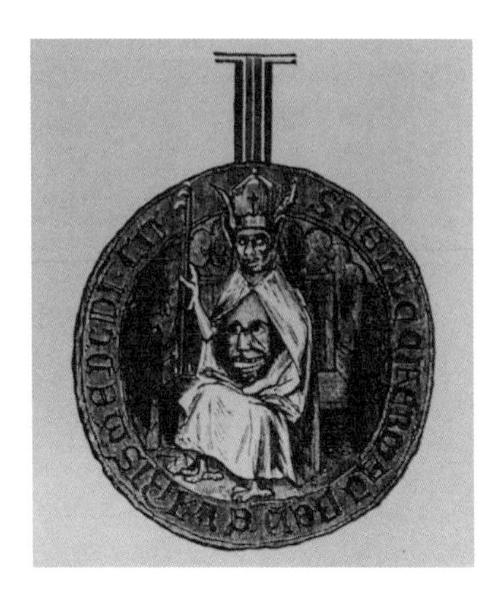

Fairies can pile inside one another by downsizing. For example, one will swallow hundreds of others just so they can all use the one bus pass.